NEGRO and WHITE

in

CONNECTICUT TOWN

by

Frank F. Lee

Associate Professor of Sociology
Adelphi College, Garden City, N. Y.

COLLEGE AND UNIVERSITY PRESS
New Haven, Connecticut

Preface

This study is based upon the writer's unpublished doctoral dissertation, "Race Relations in a Small New England Industrial Town: A Cultural Study in Social Control," Yale University, 1953. Three articles based on this material have been published: "The Race Relations Pattern by Areas of Behavior in a Small New England Town," *American Sociological Review*, Vol. 18, No. 2, April 1954, pp. 138-143; "Social Controls in the Race Relations Pattern of a Small New England Town," *Social Forces*, Vol. 33, No. 1, October 1954, pp. 36-40; and "A Cross-Institutional Comparison of Northern and Southern Race Relations," *Sociology and Social Research*, Vol. 42, No. 3, January-February 1958, pp. 185-191.

The name of the town has been disguised, and the names of all individuals, places, and local organizations referred to have been fictionalized where necessary.

Thanks are due to the citizens of Connecticut Town who befriended me during the course of my stay there and on subsequent visits. In particular I should like to thank all the informants who gave so generously of their time, as well as the many friends who aided me in establishing contacts and in learning about the town.

Most especially I am grateful to Professor Maurice R. Davie of Yale University for his constant encouragement and assistance and for the many hours he spent with me both at the time of the study and in years since. Professor Charles Woodhouse of the University of California at Riverside has been of inestimable help in the rewriting of the original manuscript. Professor John Sirjamaki, formerly of Yale University and now at the University of Minnesota, and Professor John Ellsworth of Yale University also gave much assistance at the time of the study. I should like to stress, however, that the finished product is exclusively my own work, and that I alone must take the responsibility for it.

Miss June Hanson and Mrs. Elizabeth Lewis of the University of California at Riverside, were most cooperative and devoted in their typing of the manuscript.

Finally, I should like to thank my wife, Margaret, for her constant striving for readable English, as well as for her other criticisms and suggestions.

F. F. L.

Contents

I. Introduction   11

II. Background of Race Relations in Connecticut
    Town   23

III. Race Relations in Connecticut Town, 1950-1952   39

IV. Processes and Techniques of Control   78

V. Summary and Interpretations   125

Appendices

    Appendix A
    Biographical Data on Negro Informants   139

    Appendix B
    Biographical Data on White Informants   147

    Appendix C
    Positions of Authority Held by White
    Informants   161

Notes   165

Annotated Bibliography   177

Index   201

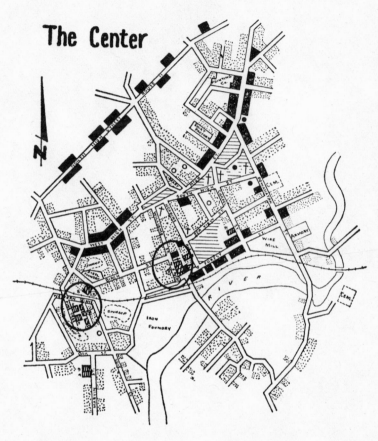

The Center

Legend:

- O School
- ▨ Negro Buildings
- **13** No. of Inhabitants per Dwelling Unit
- ⑬ No. of Inhabitants per Building
- ◯ Segregated Area

- ● Municipal Building
- † Church
- ■ Business
- ▦ Residence
- ◩ Parks and Greens

CHAPTER ONE

Introduction

The United States has long been characterized by an established pattern of race relations involving whites and Negroes. This situation has attracted the attention of many social scientists, among others, and a large amount of literature dealing with the subject, both practical and theoretical, has appeared.

Most sociological studies have dealt either with the South,[1] or with Northern urban centers,[2] or have surveyed the field as a whole.[3] The Southern pattern of subordination of the Negro, both urban and rural, is well known. Less well known is the fact that there is also an established, though different, pattern of subordination in Northern cities, while least known is the race relations situation in small communities like Connecticut Town.[4] As one local Negro remarked, "People who write about the race problem write only of the big cities or the South. They never write about these small towns, and nobody knows how bad [or good] they are."

We therefore wished to study an area that is usually thought to be "liberal" in terms of race relations, but which has been generally ignored to date. It was also felt that race relations might possibly take a different form where only small numbers of Negroes were involved, and where they lived in the comparative intimacy of a small town.

This report concerns a 1951-1952 field study of Negro-white relations in a small New England town. This study had two objectives. The first objective was to determine the "place" of the Negro in the community. We wished to discover what the race relations pattern was and whether this pattern varied from one area of behavior to another.[5] In other words, we tried to determine the extent of Negro subordination and exclusion, or conversely, the degree of Negro participation, in the different areas of behavior relative to white people in the community.

Secondly, this investigation aimed to ascertain the means of controlling and perpetuating the race relations pattern. We wished to find out what processes of social control operate to keep Negroes "in their place." Many of the obvious formal and institutionalized informal means of control have been extensively investigated in the South and in some of our large Northern cities. In the North, however, we do not generally find the thinly veiled threat of violence against Negroes for getting "out of place." Legally they have equal status, and the spoken values of the dominant white population emphasize equality. Nevertheless, Negroes do "stay in their place," and we must ask, "What is their 'place'?" and "What keeps them there?"

Our interest in the means used by one group to control another group further required that we examine the town's social organization to see what conditions operate there to maintain the present pattern of race relations. In so doing we were interested not only in the values, folkways, and mores of the community, but also in the socioeconomic characteristics of the subordinate group relative to the dominant group. Finally we wanted to learn whether any actions or attitudes of the subordinate group contributed to the perpetuation of its present status.

One further note should be added. In any situation of separation between racial, religious, or nationality groups such as exists in the United States, members of the dominant group (in this case, the whites) have to learn their "place" too, and controls also operate to keep them there. For purposes of simplification, however, this study will stress the Negro's "place" and how it is maintained.

In specifying the means by which the Negro is kept "in his place," we are observing certain processes of social control. But we describe and analyze these processes within a different frame of reference from that commonly connoted by this concept. Previous studies of social control have sought to explain why individuals consistently behave in accordance with the expectations of other people. In the attempt to analyze conformity, reference has been made to the mechanisms employed to make the individual aware of the approval or disapproval of his fellows,[6] to the effects and influence of socialization,[7] and to the traditions which legitimize the imposition of sanctions to punish or reward.[8]

By and large, however, the significance of these factors has been considered on such a high level of generality as to postulate a dichotomy between the "individual" on the one hand and the "group" or "society" on the other. Thus most of these writers have not seemed to recognize the variable social contexts within which such factors operate in a more limited situation. Such an approach has tended to ignore the plurality of groups in a large society and the extent to which the behavior of their members is conditioned by the interrelations of groups as such. Even where the group as well as the individual nature of social control has been specifically considered, the analysis has seemed inadequate as regards the interracial situation. The white techniques for keeping the Negro "in his place" have been defined, but the concept of social control has not been sufficiently elaborated even in the standard studies on Negro-white relations.

Two conceptual modifications of the theory of social control thus appear to be necessary. In the first place, the general theory neglects such impersonal factors as differences in cultural and regional backgrounds, behavior patterns, living conditions, relative numbers, and so forth. All these factors limit any group's opportunity to participate fully in community life. Secondly, while the general theory mentions the controls any group exercises over its members, the main emphasis seems to be on the controls or pressures emanating from the dominant group, while the possibility of self-imposed control by the subordinate group is largely ignored. To be sure, some social psychologists have stressed the conditioning of the individual, but conditioning on a group basis has been largely overlooked.[9]

If this reasoning is valid, we can then generalize that the unidimensional controls which operate directly from the dominant group to the subordinate group are actually, save possibly in times of conflict, only a small part of the control factors in the total situation. Aside from this one-to-one aspect of control, we anticipated that at least three other types of controls would be found. The first of these would be the impersonal factors such as the relative socioeconomic position of the two groups. The second would be the controls exerted by the dominant group upon its own members, reinforced by their rationalizations. And the third important control factor would be the attitudes held by the members of the subordinate group: the acceptance of the pattern, the acquiescence in it—a type of self-imposed control. All of these, it was felt, should be considered as an integral part of the concept of social control.

Social control, for the purposes of this study, therefore refers to the pressures exerted on Negroes by impersonal forces, as well as by whites and by the Negro community. All of these make for conformity to the established rules and social norms. Our definition includes, further, the sum total of techniques, mechanisms, rules, sanctions, folkways, mores, and processes whereby a community, in this case Connecticut Town, attempts to secure the conformity of all its members to its norms and patterns.

Site

Connecticut Town, the site of the research project, is a small, suburban, vacation, and industrial town located ten miles from an important urban center of over 125,000 population (hereafter referred to as "Central City"). Bought over 300 years ago from a local Indian tribe, in 1950 Connecticut Town had a population of just over 10,000 people,[10] of whom, by the author's count, 170 were Negroes, or a mere 1.5 to 2 percent.

Connecticut Town's distribution of gainful workers compares in percentage distribution rather closely with that of the United States as a whole, and with New England and Connecticut in particular. Four out of a hundred are professional persons, and sixteen out of a hundred are proprietors, managers, or officials of some kind. Clerks make up 14 percent of the labor force, and 63 percent are workers (30 percent skilled, 13 percent semiskilled, and 20 percent unskilled). Connecticut Town therefore is an occupationally balanced town, although the vast majority of the Negroes who are gainfully employed do unskilled or semiskilled work.

Ethnically and religiously Connecticut Town is also similar to other small towns of the New England and Connecticut area, both historically and in present-day terms. Up to 1784 when an Episcopal Church was organized, it was almost exclusively British and Congregational. A Baptist Church was founded in 1839. The dilution of the old Yankee stock began with the arrival of the Irish in the late 1840's, and a Roman Catholic Church was established soon afterward. The next arrivals were the Swedes and Finns in 1881 who brought their Lutheran religion with them. Then came the Austro-Hungarian nationalities, and around 1900 the Italians. As of the time of the study the major ethnic groups were: British or Yankee, 35 to 40 percent; Swedes, 14 percent; Italians, 13 percent; Slavs, 13 percent; and

Irish, 10 percent. As mentioned earlier, Negroes came to 1.5 or 2 percent.

On a religious basis, the town is divided nearly equally between Protestants and Roman Catholics. This is a comparatively new development. The slight Protestant majority consists of 47 percent Congregational, 22 percent Lutheran, 18 percent Episcopal, and 13 percent Baptist.[11] The colored population, with minor exceptions, belongs to the African Methodist Episcopal Zion Church. The latter also has a score or so of Central City Negroes on its rolls, most of whom at one time lived in Connecticut Town.

The heart of the town, and its main residential and business area, is the Center, otherwise known as the Borough. As in most New England towns, the Green is the center of activity. Located there are the Town Hall and three churches, the oldest and most austere of which is the Congregational Church, dominating the entire area from its little knoll. In addition there is an old semicolonial building called the Academy—the town's oldest public structure, used by the Congregational Church as a Sunday School. To the east of the knoll and slightly below it are the Town Hall and the attractive Episcopal Church. To the west and standing on the site of the old whipping post (sic) is the Baptist Church, white with green shutters and a unfinished steeple, attractively flood-lit at night.

The north side of the Green, which is triangular in shape, is bounded by High Street and is filled with the typically uninspiring American storefronts. Most of these are two-story buildings, consisting of grocery, hardware, clothing, drug, and liquor stores, law and real estate offices, a bank, and a few apartments. South High Street, which comprises another of the Green's three sides, consists of high-prestige private homes occupied exclusively by people of North European descent. It also has an attractive high school, a new and pleasant-appearing funeral home, and a dilapidated combination Masonic Temple and Community Hall. On the Green's eastern side is Powahatan Street with its private residences and attractive stores, including a comparatively new bank and post office.

South of the Green are two blocks filled mostly by private homes. Beyond them is the town's main industrial area, the railroad tracks, and the river. To the west and facing each other across High Street are the Roman Catholic Church with its several structures, all in Spanish-style architecture, and the Memorial Library, an uncommonly fine library for so small a town.

The oldest, largest, and most important industry is an iron and steel foundry (hereafter referred to as the Iron Foundry), employing almost 900 workers. Nearly half of these are Negro, most of them from out of town. Its nearest rival in size of labor force is a wire mill company (hereafter referred to as the Wire Mill) with around 400 workers. None of them is Negro. In addition to these two industries, there are four small industries or businesses of sufficient size to merit attention. The Crucible Steel Foundry is located in this same general area. The Shirt Factory, the Toy Factory, and the Pattern and Foundry Works are found elsewhere in town, the latter two being on the main traffic route on the town's eastern outskirts. Each these firms employs, or has employed in the fairly recent past, a few Negro workers.

This central area, plus the one or two square miles of surrounding territory, is the locale of the major part of this study. In addition to it, and also a part of Connecticut Town, are four political and residential subdivisions which are rather loosely defined. Apple Valley and Pilgrim Head, once exclusively summer resorts, have now become commuting suburbs of Central City. Rocky Ledge, once economically self-sufficient due to its stone quarry, now depends on the summer tourist trade for its well-being. Beach Haven, closest to Central City, and another of its commuting suburbs, is the last of these semiautonomous units with a few of its own civic and social institutions. With the exception of Pilgrim Head, an exclusive and mainly upper-class area, the town as a whole is characterized by middle-class uniformity.

Here then is Connecticut Town, in many ways a typical small New England town with a predominantly middle-class orientation and few instances of great wealth or poverty. Industrialized and in some respects quite modern, it still operates under the old town-meeting form of government and a Board of Selectmen. It is largely independent of Central City economically, although still relying on it for most leisure-time activities outside of the local movie theater, the various beaches, and the wealthy Apple Valley Country Club. This dependence on Central City is particularly true in the case of the colored population.

Method

In gathering data, Dollard says, "Method must conform to material and not vice versa."[12] Thus, general headings, comprehending broad areas of behavior, were set up corresponding to certain interests common to most people in a community. Most people in Connecticut Town, as in any American community, have an enduring interest in their residential areas and homes, their jobs, the children's education, social relationships, religion, politics, and public facilities. While no two people may have the same emotions about any of them, or share the same prejudices, predispositions, aspirations, and ideals, there comes to be a kind of least common denominator of behavior and attitudes. Hence, people can be interviewed and the racial pattern and the processes of control can be observed in terms of the community's major activities: housing, jobs (including union activities), education, social and religious life, politics, and the use of public facilities.

Information on both the degree of Negro participation and the control processes was obtained on this basis, and the race relations pattern is presented in these terms. The processes of control, however, are analyzed separately, cutting across the areas of behavior.

Three techniques were used in gathering the information: (1) participant observation (the author lived in the town throughout the two years of the study); (2) interviews conducted on an open-ended basis with the assistance of schedules; and (3) examination of documentary materials. All three approaches were directed toward answering two main questions. First, what is the Negro's "place" relative to the white? Is there a separate "place" for him, and if so, what is it? Secondly, what forces operate upon the whites and Negroes to maintain separation?

Contact with both the white and Negro communities was made in the seven months prior to the beginning of field work. During this period every effort was made to inform people of the author's research project, and his status as a Yale graduate research student was soon established. When the actual field work began, much pertinent information had already been acquired and recorded. It provided a foundation on which the interviews were built. Most of this information was unsolicited, having been obtained in the normal course of conversation and participation in local affairs.

In the Negro community the initial and most important contact was the Negro minister and his wife who became good friends of the researcher and his wife. We frequently attended their church for services and suppers, and came to know the various members of the congregation. Contacts were also established with those nonchurch Negroes living in the general neighborhood of our home. Acquaintanceship with the rest had to wait until interviewing commenced.

White contacts developed over a longer period of time and

were characterized by a more natural rather than a planned or forced cultivation. Several of these subsequent interviewees became our good friends, and they helped to establish relations with other persons in positions of authority, many of whom were also interviewed.

The interviews were conducted in an open-ended fashion for several reasons. First, since the author was more interested in qualitative than quantitative material, this techinque would be more revealing than any other. Secondly, the scope of the material to be covered was too great for such a precise technique as structured questionnaires. Finally, in delicate interviews of this sort, good rapport is mandatory if the findings are to be valid; and this would have been endangered had the schedules always been in sight. The schedules were therefore devised to serve as outline guides in the interviews, and to enable the pertinent and important data to be recorded concisely.

For both whites and Negroes the interview technique varied as conditions seemed to demand, and the author sought to give as little direction as possible. Everything was done to make the atmosphere relaxed and congenial. The schedules aimed only to assist the author's memory and to focus the interviews in order that detailed information could be obtained and the interviews not unduly prolonged. The schedules were memorized by the researcher because it was foreseen that in a few instances some informants, usually Negro, would refuse to talk if the researcher were taking notes. When this happened all paraphernalia was put away in favor of a completely informal chat. Many of the interviews were thus extended although they were still controlled in terms of the researcher's image of the schedule. Most informants cooperated willingly in giving their time and in answering all questions. Immediately following every interview a verbatim record was made of all that had been discussed. In no case was a complete stenographic account made of an interview due to limitation on speed of writing and to the fact that some informants talked more easily when no notes were being taken. Quotations are used wherever possible, but cannot be guaranteed to be completely accurate.

Five months were spent in this field work, two of them being devoted to the Negro group. The Negro universe was established as consisting of all Negro residents over twelve years of age, a total of 143 persons. Of these, 83 were chosen at random for interviewing, although attempts were made to include at least one member of each household. In all cases contacts were made personally in view of the known Negro suspicion of whites, particularly when being questioned. The manner in which the interviewees greeted the reseacher ran the gamut of extremes. Generally they were cooperative, and in only five instances was an interview unconditionally refused. Unfortunately, four of the refusals came from the only Negro secretaries living in Connecticut Town; these women all worked in Central City. These refusals limited our complete understanding of the local job situation. The 78 who were interviewed comprised members of every Negro household save one. The Negro group was thus substantially covered, and each member was interviewed regarding all areas of behavior. Most of these interviews lasted one and one-half hours.

Since it was impossible to cover the entire white community, 105 persons were chosen for interviews. They were selected on the basis of positions of authority and/or prestige found in each area of behavior. The people who filled these positions were the ones who might logically be assumed to know most about the practices and policies of that area. They included real estate operators and property owners; factory owners, personnel directors, foremen, and union leaders; school officials and teachers; ministers, vestrymen, and other church leaders; political leaders and holders of public office; and managers or proprietors of stores, restaurants, and other public facilities. From this pool of potential interviewees about 17 persons were selected at random for each area of behavior. Since only those areas of behavior where the informants held positions of authority were covered in these individual interviews, the white schedules were much more abbreviated than the Negro schedules. The average interview lasted a half hour. In many cases, the informant was questioned regarding several areas of behavior, as in the case of one who owned a business, was a member of the school board, and chairman of the local Rotary club. He was interviewed in terms of housing, jobs, education, and social and religious activities. Most contacts were made by telephone and in only two instances were there refusals. The reception by the informants was almost invariably friendly, interested, and cooperative.

The examination of documentary materials was necessary because the race relations patterns and the processes of social control in any community have their bases in the community's past. To make these patterns and processes intelligible, their history must be known. It was thus necessary to examine the old town records and the back files of the local newspaper.

Let us now look at a brief history of Connecticut Town from its earliest beginnings up to 1950.

CHAPTER TWO

Background of Race Relations in Connecticut Town

Before delving directly into the existing Negro-white relations in Connecticut Town, it is necessary to examine briefly the relationships that have existed in the past between the white and nonwhite populations, there and in New England. As is usually the case in culture history, these relationships molded and influenced the relationship patterns of the present day. For convenience we shall divide our time sequence into three periods: 1637-1900, 1900-1914, and 1914-1950. The first evidence of slavery in New England dates from 1637. The year 1900 is the earliest date in the memory of the present Negro population, and is approximately the time when they began to arrive in Connecticut Town. Finally, 1914 is the beginning of the heavy Negro migration to Connecticut Town as part of the general northward movement stimulated by World War I.

1637-1900

The first mention of slavery in New England, in 1637, involved not Negroes but Indians. At that time Massachusetts and Connecticut soldiers decimated and captured the Pequot Indians, following which the women and children were enslaved and the men sold into bondage outside the colonies.[1] This all took place one year before Connecticut Town was bought from the local Indian tribe and seven years before it was settled.

Negro slavery in New England dates from 1638 when

Negroes were first introduced,[2] and appears to have existed in Connecticut as early as 1639.[3] It is also said to have been practiced in Central City Colony, of which Connecticut Town was a part, by 1644.[4] Although there were only 1,000 Negroes in all New England by 1700,[5] they were sufficiently numerous for laws to be passed regulating many of their activities. Over the years in Connecticut, Negroes were restricted in freedom of movement, use of liquor, striking or defaming whites, flight or theft, residence in towns, purchase of land, business activity, and military service.[6] Furthermore, they were generally not allowed to vote on church matters and were customarily segregated in the congregations.[7] And yet with all these repressive measures, slavery in New England and Connecticut—which had the most stringent laws in the area regulating Negroes and slavery—was considerably milder than elsewhere in colonial America.[8] Democratic relationships between masters and slaves were not uncommon in rural Connecticut, and laws were passed providing "for their proper treatment and later for their ultimate freedom."[9]

The point to be noted here is that "Slavery was part of the cultural pattern of 17th and 18th century . . . New England. . . . The case of Connecticut is typical; slavery in that colony was never established by the law, but the recognition accorded it by statute and by the Courts was such 'that it may be said to have been established by law.' "[10] Of course, much of this legality was mere verbiage, and more often than not the law, including measures both favorable and unfavorable to Negroes, was not enforced. For example, despite the restrictions on Negroes in military service, dating from 1660 to as late as 1784, Negroes fought in both King George's War (1742-1748) and the French and Indian War (1756-1763).[11] During this time the number of Negroes in Connecticut remained small, somewhere between 700 and 1,500 for the years 1715 to 1730.[12]

There were no radical changes in the status of the Connecticut Negro until 1774 when, with a Negro population of 6,464 or 3.2 percent of the total and the largest number of Negroes in any New England state,[13] Connecticut forbade further importation of slaves.[14] Ten years later the state abolished slavery, the rest of New England following suit by 1790.[15] By the latter date, when the first federal census was taken, Connecticut's Negro population had decreased by 16.1 percent and was down to 5,419 or 2.3 percent of the population, still the largest number in the New England area.[16]

The change in the legal status of Negroes in Connecticut in 1784 did not bring them any important social or civil advantages. For many years they continued to be recognized as a distinct social caste, segregated in churches, schools, and many public facilities. And suffrage was withheld until after the Civil War, the only instance of a New England state being so restrictive.

Connecticut Town, of course, shared this over-all pattern. The first recorded instance of Negro slavery there was in 1699,[17] and the last mention of it was in 1767.[18] By 1774 the Negro population was estimated at 113 out of a total of 1,938.[19] But, presumably because of the abolition of slavery and other changing conditions, these numbers decreased to only 67 by 1800.[20] Despite the many disabilities under which he lived, the Connecticut Town Negro from about 1800 on could lead a fairly full life. He owned land even though apart from whites and,[21] following the repeal in 1838 of the "Prudence Crandall" law requiring segregated Negro education, the school system developed as one institution where social discrimination was largely held in abeyance.

Negroes continued to live in Connecticut Town throughout the ensuing years, though apparently in decreasing numbers. With the end of the nineteenth century there probably were no more than six or seven families still there.

Among them was one individual who was reported to have had a Negro father and white mother. As remarked by the oldest living Negro resident at the time of the study (hereafter referred to as Mrs. Hart), who arrived in 1898 as a nineteen-year-old bride, he "did not associate with us other Negroes much as a result of this unfortunate fact." Of the others, one married a white man and left town, and another had a Hindu husband and Negro daughter as well as an adopted white daughter.

1900-1914

Until World War I there was no noticeable change in the number of Negroes; the 1910 Census listed only nineteen.[22] Of these only four were males of voting age. There was little discrimination according to Mrs. Hart. If true, this seems largely to have been due to their small numbers and to the fact that most of them were old and established members of the community, an important factor in conservative New England. For example, there was apparently no difficulty in getting a home or in buying land save for their own financial capabilities.

Yet there was differential status for them. Job discrimination was not visible, but the only Negro ever offered the job of foreman at the Iron Foundry before 1950 turned it down because "he thought too many whites would object" (Mrs. Hart). Negro women also worked at the Iron Foundry at that time. The only other jobs they held were in domestic service; this was at least partially due to their lack of training and interest rather than to discriminatory practices as such.

The same held true, generally speaking, for the schools. Though nonsegregated, they apparently discriminated against Negro students upon occasion. Most of the difficulty was attributed by Negro residents to the Superintendent and to recent immigrant groups, particularly the Poles and Lithuanians, whose children caused a considerable number of fights and stonings. The situation was eventually cleared up by the active intervention of one of the town's leading citizens who threatened to "horsewhip any children who caused any more trouble" (Mrs. Hart). In any case, Negro children did not generally participate in school social activities, and, of course, there were no Negro teachers.

Social relations with whites seem to have been good, if paternalistic. As an example of this, one excellent Negro tennis player was allowed the use of the Country Club courts to keep in form, but he was not permitted to join the club. Otherwise, the Negro families were liked and respected, but played a limited part in community life.

In church membership most Negroes were Congregationalists. However, though Negro children participated in Sunday School on the same basis as white children, few Negro adults ever attended church; when they did they sat segregated in the balcony. Nor did they participate in any of the social activities of the parish. The same was true for the few Negroes in other churches, both Protestant and Roman Catholic. This was probably because they sensed the general white attitude, as expressed by one of the white old-timers: "Of course they would have been welcome, but don't you think they are happier with their own color?" (WI-78).* Yet the Negroes claimed to be unaware of discrimination.

As for political behavior, there was scant Negro participation beyond the discussion stage, presumably because of their withdrawal for lack of interest and ability. And with regard to public facilities, evidence of discrimination was also lacking. All facilities, with one or two possible exceptions such as the barber and beauty shops, were probably

---

*In the interests of brevity all Negro and white informants will hereafter be referred to respectively as NI and WI, followed by their identification number. The keys to these numbers will be found in Appendices A and B, respectively.

open to those who could afford them. But it cannot be said with certainty whether they utilized these services in Connecticut Town or went instead to Central City.

1914-1950

Strains in Negro-white relations began to appear after the arrival of southern Negroes brought in by the Iron Foundry as common laborers during 1915-1916. Several factors seemed to be responsible for this, the first of which was the sudden increase in their numbers. The Negro population more than doubled from 1910 to 1920 when a total of forty was reported.[23] Most of them were single men, or at least did not bring their wives with them. By 1930 the Negro population had nearly tripled, to 110.[24] Most of these increases were the direct result of the Iron Foundry's hiring policy.

Secondly, most of the migrants were quite low in cultural and socioeconomic status, which depressed still further the level of the Negro community. According to popular report, both from white and Negro, the new immigrants were prone to knife fights and heavy drinking. The whites reacted to this by so categorizing all Negroes.

Finally, as a corollary to the above two factors, there was the additional one mentioned earlier, i.e., the premium placed in New England upon being an old and established resident whom everyone knows and likes. The new influx destroyed this pattern for the Negro community.

Overt discrimination was not evident in the first part of this period, and the earlier patterns carried over for some time. By the middle 1920's, however, a change had taken place. In the field of housing, for example, a policy had become fixed "to keep the colored colony pretty much confined to Western Avenue and Windy Lane, as well as the lower part of Williams Street" (WI-95). It became increasingly difficult for Negroes to own or rent.

The "policy" of discrimination was supported by the refusal by at least one bank to give mortgages to Negroes trying to buy residences in white areas; and by the Iron Foundry's policy of encouraging Negroes to settle in Western Avenue, an uninhabited area owned by the company. Land was offered free to any Negro who had worked at the factory for five years and was willing to build on it, with possession of the property to go to him as soon as the housing mortgage was paid off. At the same time this land was not made available to whites, although it is doubtful if any but the lowest class would have considered it. Located alongside the railroad tracks and between two swamps, only a five-minute walk from the factory, it was scarcely a desirable area in which to live.

In addition to making this land available, the Iron Foundry installed a large septic tank, a water main, two private houses, and a four-apartment building. One of the private homes was given to a Negro family " 'cause he wanted us to set an example for other Negroes: keep it clean and nice, and encourage them to have homes, too" (NI-66). These policies were not entirely successful, however, for many Negroes preferred not to move to this segregated and undesirable location.

Despite the housing restrictions, some Negro families were able to buy or rent elsewhere than in the areas prescribed for them. Most of these purchases, made during 1944-1947, were not too far distant from the Negro community. Where purchases were made in white areas far removed from the Negro settlement, they invariably took place because the Negro involved knew the white seller. As one family said, "We probably got it because we knew him. You can't buy here if you're colored unless you know people" (NI-40, 41).

Negroes like these, buying into white areas, did not usually encounter friendly white attitudes. Fighting among the children was usual at first and stoning was not unknown.

One Negro mother who settled in a white area around 1935 said that not only had her neighbors erected barriers to keep her family off their property, but others had yelled insults at them and called them names. Yet in one or two cases the white neighbors were most friendly and cooperative, even to the point of engaging in social activities with the Negroes.

It must be noted that while there was obvious discrimination and prejudice against Negroes in housing, the fault for the lack of facilities did not lie exclusively with whites. There were several instances where Negroes refused to take advantage of opportunities presented.

"My husband and I had a number of chances to buy or rent. We could have bought a house on Birch Street, just east of the Crucible Steel Foundry, but he was satisfied where he was [living in the boarding house in the segregated area]. We could also have bought the boarding house on Oak Street from the Iron Foundry, but again he didn't want it. That was in 1937. And I could have rented a beer tavern on West High Street from Goens, but my husband didn't want me to do it" (NI-36).

Job discrimination became a firmly established part of the race relations pattern during this period. No other Negroes at the Iron Foundry were offered promotions to foreman such as that earlier tendered, and Negro women were excluded from employment there early in the 1920's. The latter policy was allegedly due to friction between white and Negro women over shower and toilet facilities, and management took the easy way out. At least eight Negro women applied there for jobs between 1940-1950, and more at earlier times; all were turned down or given the "run-around." Moreover, other jobs which Negroes had not previously been qualified to fill remained closed to them despite their acquistion of new skills. Some of this may also have been due to their lack of interest in such jobs.

In at least two other instances Negroes were pushed out of jobs which they had previously held, i.e., at the Furniture Shop and the Wire Mill. The last time a Negro was employed at the Wire Mill was in 1935; not even the wartime labor shortage or antidiscriminatory legislation* changed this situation. In one or two industries, however, certain jobs and skills which had been quietly but effectively barred to them suddenly were made available during World War II. The Shirt Factory, where they had been kept out of the stitching rooms, is a good example. In addition, the Toy Factory hired six Negro women for the first time. They were kept on for several years following the war, but were all gone by 1950. Their job opportunities were also limited although relations with the white women workers were friendly. In some instances they saw a good deal of each other after working hours, going to the movies, eating, and visiting together. Some of the construction companies also hired Negroes for the first time during this era and kept them as part of the permanent working force.

Another favorable factor which arose during this period— other than the wartime labor shortage, the F.E.P.C., and the increased desire by many people to live up to democratic ideals—was the Congress of Industrial Organizations (CIO). It established locals in two plants, the United Steelworkers at the Iron Foundry and the United Clothing Workers at the Shirt Factory (USW and UCW respectively). In both these

---

*The first legislation of this sort was President Roosevelt's Executive Order 8802 issued in June 1941, establishing the Committee on Fair Employment Practice (FEPC), and his subsequent Executive Order 9346 of May 1943. These orders had important effects in introducing Negro workers to both private and government jobs previously barred to them, and were followed in July 1948 by President Truman's Executive Order 9980. This order attempted to provide machinery for implementing fair employment policy and for redressing discrimination in the federal government. In addition to these Executive Orders, FEPC legislation has been enacted by many states and cities, commencing with New York State in July 1945. Connecticut followed suit in 1947.

industries the lot of the Negro worker improved substantially, thanks to the unions, and yet the Negroes as a group showed little interest in the operation and running of the union. In some cases this was due as much to fear of losing their jobs as anything else. The one exception was a highly qualified and personable man, Samuel Johnson, who served as a vice-president of the USW in the early 1940's, until he was killed in an automobile accident while on business for the local.

The school system, by and large, was the only area of behavior where progress against discrimination was consistently made. This was accomplished by strong Negro pressure, by support from a few influential whites, and by a generally enlightened faculty. This is not to say that discrimination against colored students did not sometimes occur, and occasional name-calling was found all during this time.

Throughout this period Negroes participated equally in athletic activities. They were accepted and liked by most of their schoolmates. This was true more of the boys than the girls, who had less opportunity to win the respect of their fellows by demonstrating ability in competitive sports.

In school social activities Negroes played only a minor part; they kept largely to themselves. This was due both to their small numbers and the fact that most of them came from Southern families not culturally conditioned to act on a par with whites. With but two exceptions, one the case of a boy who later became one of the Ivy League's football greats, there was little if any social visiting between the two groups.

Most Negro students, particularly girls, did not attend social events such as dances, at least partly because of their lower economic position. When they did attend, it was always with other Negroes, and there was little if any social interchange such as mixed dancing. White overtures were usually refused as in the case of a Negro boy invited to go

While professing a willingness to have Negroes in their churches, the whites were glad to see them go. This is seen in their support of St. Andrews, and in their remarks:

"I guess they just wanted to be by themselves and I really think it's the best thing for them. They feel better, they're better off, and they really work with their own church" (WI-95).

"As more Negroes came to town they just flocked together, but there was never any incident or issue that forced them out" (WI-93).

The Negroes, likewise, were glad to become independent. As Mrs. Hart stated:

"We wanted to be with our own people. There was no discrimination about it, but you feel more free with your own church. You have a voice and can make your own plans. In the Congregational Church I never tried to speak out. I wanted to work about our own people and have a church for our children. We had always been Methodists anyway."

Other Negro informants substantiated these remarks. They said they wanted their own form of worship and songs, they did not feel at home in the white churches, and were not able to participate fully in the life of the church. As mentioned earlier, they had always sat in the gallery, one of the major reasons they eventually broke away.

So in religious participation we note a specific instance of a social gap between whites and Negroes, mainly the result of socioeconomic and cultural differences. The same pattern was seen in purely social relations. More than one Negro admitted that the only whites he knew were his boss and employer, and that he could not converse with them because they did not have the same interests. Most of the children were also caught in this pattern. Neither the Boy Scouts nor Girl Scouts ever discriminated against colored children, but both developed segregated units owing to two factors. One was a desire on the part of influential Central

City Negroes to form Negro units. In the Girls Scouts, for example, according to their Connecticut Town founder:

"Shortly after they were formed, a Mrs. Lula Mae Mc-Williams, a colored lady from Central City who was on the District Council, suggested that the colored children would be better off by themselves. She came out, talked to them at St. Andrews and helped them organize a separate group. It was moderately successful only, and the colored parents did absolutely nothing for it. I don't feel it was the right thing to do though it may have been for Central City. If they had stayed with the white troops, I think they would have been more stimulated to do their best and would have found it more interesting" (WI-95).

The other factor was that eventually the Scout troops came to be organized under the aegis of the churches. As a result, nearly all the colored were members of a troop exclusively their own since few of them were members of churches other than St. Andrews. It should be noted that the Scout movement never really aroused the interest and support of the Negro community.

The only adult and adolescent groups where Negroes were accepted as equals and which were not associated with the churches were the Hi-Y and the Town Band. In both, those who were interested and qualified participated to the extent they desired. By and large, however, only the members of two of the oldest Negro families plus occasional other individuals took advantage of these opportunities.

One other individual, of Portuguese extraction, belonged to the American Legion but took little part in its activities. His wife was an active member of the Ladies Auxiliary. She got along well with most of the other women although some individuals never accepted her. Other Negroes might have become members of the Legion, too; yet, when they applied they were told that while they could join if they wished, they probably would not be happy there.

In no other social or religious organizations were Negroes present. None applied, and none would have been admitted had he done so except in one or two unusual cases. This will be understood when one considers their cultural and socioeconomic level in comparison with the whites, with regard to various clubs covered in this study: service clubs, secret organizations, veterans organizations, fraternal organizations, social clubs, musical organizations, and even such ones as the Red Cross and Visiting Nurse Association (VNA).

Negroes participated even less in politics than in other areas of behavior, only one or two showing enough interest to work for the two political parties, or to join their respective clubs. Negroes were almost exclusively Democratic after 1932, having overcome their fear of reprisals by the Iron Foundry as well as having been influenced by other more obvious factors such as the Depression. As for the courts, they had a good bit of trouble with Negroes in the 1930's and early 1940's, largely due to lack of employment and housing, plus the lack of controls emanating from the absence of Negro leadership. With respect to the volunteer Fire Department, the two times when Negroes were invited to join they spurned the overtures. They were not interested in the prestige, and allegedly rejected it because of low pay, the hours, and the inconveniences. None was ever solicited for the Police Department, though similar overtures made here would probably have been rejected, too.

Finally, discrimination in public facilities definitely increased during this period though it never became an overwhelming problem. It was most obvious in the businesses depending upon social contact or personal services: barber shops, bars, beaches, motels, clothing stores. The barber shops and bars were the worst. However, in some cases Negroes voluntarily segregated themselves by using similar facilities in Central City. This tendency will be discussed in greater detail later.

This historical review of race relations in Connecticut Town has shown, in the first two periods covered, a shift away from the formal institution of slavery to a transitional phase in which segregation and discrimination were relatively unstructured. The last period shows a reversal of this trend with increasing segregation and the beginning of a new institutionalization of Negro-white relations. These developments seem related to Negro numbers, both actual and percentagewise, though this is more obvious in the years since World War I. From 1910, which marked the low point in the size of the Negro community, their numbers and percentage have increased, and racial differences have become more important. It should also be noted that, save for the slavery period, the Negro has not been firmly or permanently entrenched in the life of the community; compared to the white population he has been quite transient.[25] Discounting the factor of color, however, the few Negro old-timers have been accepted much as have white old-timers. But Negro newcomers, even more than white newcomers, have had great difficulties in adjusting and making an acceptable "place" for themselves. We shall now see what the "place" of the Negro is today.

CHAPTER THREE

Race Relations in Connecticut Town, 1950-1952

We can see the present race relations pattern most clearly by briefly describing and analyzing each of the following areas of behavior in turn: housing, jobs and unions, schools, social and religious activities, politics, and public facilities.

Housing

Negro housing in Connecticut Town is very bad. As one of the more influential and sympathetic white politicians said, "Housing for Negroes is the sore spot of the town and the crux of the entire problem. The people here are willing to take their money, but not to let them live here" (WI-55).

As can be seen from both the end paper map and the map on page 9, Negroes are concentrated within one or two blocks of the railroad tracks and their usual place of work, the Iron Foundry.[1] This area is not solidly Negro, however, but has numerous white families scattered throughout most of it.

Within the encircled areas, which can be considered the "segregated" area, are twenty-two Negro dwelling units in thirteen buildings. Here live one hundred people, or nearly three-fifths of the town's Negroes. Seven buildings, with eight residential units, are owned by Negroes; they have forty-five inhabitants, both owners and tenants. The other six buildings with fourteen units have fifty-five inhabitants. None of the buildings has more than four rooms, and most have three.

Outside the "segregated" area, and generally quite widely scattered, the remaining seventy-odd Negroes live in eleven dwelling units and buildings. Eight of these are Negro-owned for a total of sixteen owned homes. The rest of the Negroes live and work as domestic servants in private white homes, largely in Apple Valley. In addition one family owns a second plot of twenty acres of woodland in Rocky Ledge, and a nonlocal relative of another family has a lot in Pilgrim Head.

The average monthly rent of the thirteen families which divulged this information is roughly $19.85, both inside and outside the "segregated" area. The average number of rooms per person is just over one; for the twenty families which answered this question, there was no noticeable variation between owned and rented homes.

The condition of the homes is one of the first things to attract one's attention. Two comparisons can be drawn. First, with respect to those buildings where interviews were held, nine of the twelve buildings within the "segregated" area were in need of major repairs as against four among the eight buildings outside this area, in other words 75 percent as opposed to 50 percent. Secondly, regarding the differences between homes owned and rented in which there were interviews, out of a total of thirteen owned buildings, seven were in good condition as opposed to none among the seven rented homes. In other words, of the twenty buildings where interviews were held, only seven were in good condition. All were Negro-owned and four were outside the "segregated" area. As one Negro, a two-year college man, said, "Whites owning homes where Negroes live aren't interested in keeping them up, but Negroes who own their own homes take care of them" (NI-10).

A somewhat extreme, but not atypical, case of the treatment given Negro tenants by white landlords is seen in the following remarks:

"We live here in an old store. We have no bath, toilet or hot water. All we have is cold running water, and we put that in ourselves. Before that we had to lug it over from next door. The owner doesn't keep the property up and won't make any repairs. He wouldn't even give us the paint to fix it up. We had to buy that ourselves, too" (NI-14, 15).

But more significant than the physical housing conditions are the questions: what can Negroes do about their housing, where and how easily can they buy or rent, and what kinds of discrimination do they encounter?

Most residential areas in town are covered by some type of restrictive covenants even though they cannot legally be enforced;[2] only occasionally can Negroes buy elsewhere than in the "segregated" area. More than that, there are no homes to buy *inside* this area; even there whites outnumber Negroes and are determined to prevent them from spreading further. Thus Negroes trying to buy homes face an impossible situation; about all they can do is build on the Iron Foundry's "segregated" land. Renting is no better. Not only are rents unreasonably high for the facilities available, but the opportunity to share a building with a white family, as is done by many whites, is limited to only one white family which will allow it. A few Negro quotations may help to illustrate the above remarks:

"I have to live with my mother-in-law because we can't find anybody who will sell to us. We are all sort of crammed together around the Iron Foundry and the railroad tracks" (NI-78 left for Central City with his family before the study was completed).

"Housing is bad and hard to get. If we weren't living way out here [on Foote's Island Road], and in a barn at that, we wouldn't be here at all. Originally they tried to put us off in a swamp, but even that was too close to some white homes and people objected" (NI-64, 65).

"The housing situation is bad. There's just no place for

colored. Why, when Mrs. Miller's house burned, she had to leave town because no one would rent or sell to her. They won't even rent you garages" (NI-20, 21).

This is not to say that all, or even most, Negroes have taken what might be considered sufficient steps to obtain housing. Said one middle-aged woman, "I don't find too much housing discrimination and what there is they bring on themselves in large measure. There were lots of homes for sale and rent around 1940 which Negroes could have bought but didn't" (NI-34). So while there is some discrimination against Negroes, at least part of their housing problem is due to their desire to live together and not take chances. As noted earlier, since 1944 a few Negroes have bought properties from whites in nonsegregated areas. If one could buy, others who complain but who do not try might also be successful.

Aside from unusual cases of this type, there are additional ways in which Negroes might get property. The first, which has never been tried, is to "pass" for white or to have some white friend buy for them. Another is to find a situation where a white wants to bring Negroes into the neighborhood, possibly to spite his neighbors. One Negro couple had such an opportunity in Beach Haven but lacked the drive to press it to a successful conclusion, at least partly because of the distance from the rest of the Negro community. Still a third way is to watch closely whenever other Negroes buy into white areas and take advantage of the situation as whites panic and move out.

White feelings about Negro housing can be seen in the fate of a proposed state-aided municipal housing project. When first suggested in 1950, Connecticut Town picked a committee to look into it.

"They had a hard time getting a piece of land to locate it on due to the nondiscriminatory clause in the bill. The local Negro minister was put on the committee to represent the Negroes, and that killed it. They couldn't get any land. Finally, however, some was obtained, very cheaply, at a good price, eighteen acres on the Rocky Ledge Road. It was all approved by the state authorities and then they called a Town Meeting, and Mr. Beach showed up with ten to eighteen Negroes. That really killed it. They even brought the lame, the halt, and the blind. It was all most unfortunate, for it is doubtful if any Negro families would have been even eligible in terms of veterans' preferences and financial requirements" (WI-66).

The project was resubmitted to the voters in the fall of 1951 and was defeated just as decisively. The results of the affair are Republican accusations that the Democrats played politics, and the arousing of latent racial resentment. As two Negroes said:

"Look at what happened to the Housing Project. There's a good example of what the situation is like. They told Evans that if the colored couldn't find a place to live, they could do so in his backyard" (NI-40).

"We tried to get a Housing Project some time ago, but they said, 'Let them go in the woods and live.' They wouldn't even listen to us. What kind of a place is it to live where they say, 'Let them go in the woods and live'?" (NI-23).

The Iron Foundry's previously mentioned housing policy has continued without change, and has been an important contributing factor in the present housing situation.[3] But it met with limited success outside of its own efforts until 1952 when two young Negro veterans decided to build on Western Avenue and put up two attractive homes. Why and how did one of them go about it?

"Finally we got this proposition here [from the Iron Foundry] and it seemed to be the most appealing. I saw the owner of it. It may seem stupid to you to have taken it, but I had a family coming on and had to find a place to live. My mother told me last time I was home that I was foolish not to even have a signed agreement. Anyway, I told my story and [the president] said he had this land to offer. He said he wasn't going to let anyone have it unless he approved of them and thought they would take care of it and fix it up. He gave us the land, but we don't get the deed until the home is paid for. We have a fifteen-year mortgage which the contractor holds, but the shop [Iron Foundry] deducts it from our pay.

"Of course, I must admit we didn't want to come here at first. I'm an American citizen and I want to feel I can live where I please. In a sense this is a segregated area, although there are white people living here, and I always insist on giving our address as Pine Tree Avenue and not as Western Avenue. I don't like the idea of living in a segregated area, and I'm sure the owner wouldn't sell to whites, but what can I do about it?" (NI-60).

The Iron Foundry's policy, however, has not saved it from criticism. Most Negroes criticize it for supporting segregation, while many whites and some Negroes feel that not enough is being done to provide housing for the Negro workers which it had, after all, brought in.

No description of the housing situation would be complete without further mention of the part played in the maintenance of the ecological pattern by real estate interests and the banks. As a liberal bank and real estate official said, "Negroes have a chance like a snowball in Hell of doing any sort of business with real estate companies, and especially where Pilgrim Head is concerned" (WI-66). Interviews were held with all the real estate men in town; they were frank in discussing their attitudes and policies. Briefly, these can be summed up by saying that they would never sell to Negroes in any localities which were predominantly white. In other words, Negroes trying to buy through them could only do so in "either a Negro district or on the outskirts of town where neighbors aren't too close" (WI-60).

The basic reason given was the universal argument that damage would be done to property values.[4] In fact, only one real estate man has ever been placed in the predicament of having to act in an overtly discriminatory manner. As one of them pointed out, "The owners pretty well determine the situation and generally they want to keep it white" (WI-105). In the two instances where Negroes did try to buy from real estate men, one was an out-of-towner looking for a site for a boys' camp. There was nothing available for him. In the other case, a sale was made to a local Negro with white contacts, near but not in the "segregated" area. With regard to the banks, at least one still has a discriminatory policy of refusing mortgages to Negroes desiring to move into white areas.

Negro-white neighborhood relations are generally good but limited, and are characterized by a live-and-let-live attitude. This exists mainly in those areas where both races have lived for a considerable period of time. Where Negroes move into hitherto solely white neighborhoods, they are usually greeted with some hostility. The general situation is indicated below:

"We get along just fine. Negroes take part in all charity drives and when my husband died [in 1950] they all [the whites] sent flowers, money, etc. Of course, when we first moved in here they were a little bit stuffy and unfriendly, but they soon changed" (NI-1).

"When we got this home, the neighbors acted a little hinkty [stuffy] for a while, a couple of years or so. Then they came to themselves and are good neighbors now. We get along fine, chat with them, borrow from them and vice versa, but of course we never visit each other" (NI-50).

As an example of a more extreme type of situation we have the following: "I never talk to my white neighbors, and they never talk to me" (NI-12).

Jobs and Unions

There are plenty of jobs for Negroes in Connecticut Town. But although they seem to be improving in both quality and quantity, the jobs are severely limited in some respects.[5] Let us look at each of the various job possibilities in detail.

The Iron Foundry, the largest employer of both white and colored, has two distinct employment problems. The first concerns the male workers. Out of a total work force of around 900, over 400 are Negro men of whom forty-odd live in town. The rest come mainly from Central City. By and large the Foundry shows little overt discrimination against these men. All plant facilities such as lockers, showers, and cafeteria are used equally by Negroes and whites. The problem here is, therefore, one of evaluating the differences between Negro skills and the jobs which are not only allegedly open to them but in which they actually work.

Most workers of both races claim to know of no job discrimination. One Negro employee said, "Any job they want and can fill is open to them. If there aren't any in there, it isn't discrimination but because they haven't tried or been qualified" (NI-62). There are many job areas in which Negroes are not represented, e.g., the pattern shop, galvanizing, the machine shop, the shipping room, crane operation, the coupler department, and the maintenance gang. Management admits that "we haven't encouraged Negroes to enter these jobs because of the feelings of some of the men and foremen. However, if one applied and was qualified, or if we needed a man in there and the best one was colored, we'd back him to the hilt" (WI-94).

In supervisory work there is only one Negro foreman who was appointed in 1950 after twenty-five years of service. In addition, there are Negroes supervising whites in a few other instances. It is impossible to say whether any of these are capable of being promoted to a foremanship.

The absence of Negroes from the above-mentioned job categories seems due mainly to their lack of interest, since better money can be earned in some of the unskilled and semiskilled jobs, such as moulding, than in more skilled and less dangerous and dirty jobs. Secondarily, they have not the necessary seniority, skills, or abilities, over half of them having less than an eighth grade education. Absenteeism and an alleged lack of dependability have also played a part in holding them back, as has paternalism by management in making them dependent upon it. Finally, an additional factor contributing to the low Negro occupational horizon in Connecticut Town is probably the lack of example set for the rank and file Negro workers by their "elite."[6] However, some whites and Negroes feel that the latter have been held back and barred from certain jobs, and that the above reasons are only excuses. Such truth as there is in this is probably based on the fact that much influence and power rests with the individual foreman. "If he likes Negroes, O.K. If he doesn't, too bad. All advancement and training is up to him" (NI-48).

Above the rank of foreman no position at the Foundry is open to Negroes. At present this is largely an academic question since none is qualified or has applied.

Relations between white and Negro workers are generally good if not close, although there are some whites who grumble against Negroes. Inside the factory they get on well together; outside, there is little contact between them. A few Negroes complained that "in the shop and at the plant it's 'Hi, Bill, how are you?', [but] if you see them on the streets, especially with their wives, they don't even know you" (NI-14).

The USW, CIO, does not discriminate against Negroes.[7]

They can go as far in the local union as their desires and capabilities permit. But there have been no Negro officers since the time of Samuel Johnson, and Negroes are represented on only a few committees such as the Grievance and the Negotiating. Also there are Negro shop stewards. With one or two exceptions, Negroes, like whites, attend union meetings infrequently, and it has been difficult to get them to take any union jobs.

Union social relationships are much the same as in the factory. At union meetings and picnics the two races get on well together and mix freely in all activities with no apparent friction. Many Negro members, however, stick fairly closely to one another, which is understandable in the light of neighborhood and job patterns. As before, some complain of being "cut dead on the street."

The second problem relating to the Iron Foundry concerns Negro women. None has worked there since the early 1920's. Their continued absence is the result of discrimination, as was freely admitted by the wife of one of the officials. "Yes, there's discrimination at the Foundry for colored girls" (WI-57). The alleged reasons for not hiring them have included lack of openings, the need for separate toilet facilities, and the admission by management that they did not want the problem of hiring colored women. Management claims to be trying to end this situation and to reintroduce them into the plant. It is difficult to say if this is true. For example, in the summer of 1951 a daughter of the Negro foreman applied for a job and was told there were no vacancies. A few months later, after she got a job at the Central City Telephone Company, she was told they had room for her. Whether this was a false gesture or not is hard to say but no Negro women were working at the Foundry by the end of 1952. It is not hard to imagine what would occur if one of the four qualified Negro secretaries who live in town but who work in Central City applied for a job.

The only other firm in town which hires Negroes in any number is the Shirt Factory. It employs women almost exclusively. Any jobs Negroes are capable of doing are now probably open to them, and they are found in every position except the office. At the same time, they seem not to be given training and the chance for advancement quite as readily as white girls, and the absence of Negro women in the office is apparently due to discrimination. One Negro informant said a qualified friend had applied for an opening there but had been told only that they would let her know. Nothing further was ever heard.

Relations between the two races at the Shirt Factory are characterized by a good many friendly and personal contacts. They not only get on well while at work but many of the women go out together afterwards for drinking, visiting, and eating. At the yearly Christmas dance and party given by management, "There has always been mixed dancing, and no one has ever objected or made any sort of trouble" (NI-39). These good interworker relations carry over into union life and activities (UCW, CIO). There is no discrimination there, and if no offices or other positions are held by Negroes, it is again due to their lack of interest or ability.

Several other plants and businesses in town employ Negroes, though in much smaller numbers. The Printing Company has always employed a few. In 1952 only one worked there although there had been others in the previous two years. There is no discrimination as far as management policies are concerned. A qualified Negro can advance as far as any white, outside of the immediate family which owns and runs the business. One interesting feature here is the paternalism evinced by management for its Negro employees. They are better and more leniently treated than are the whites. But such attitudes, as a rule, do not make for healthy relationships, and there is considerable white worker hostility toward Negro coworkers.

One or two Negroes began working at the Crucible Steel Company in 1951 for the first time. They are limited to heavy labor. Negroes have worked, too, at the local Laundry Company and the Bottling Company, though there is none at the latter firm today. Those employed at these two places expressed satisfaction over their treatment and said relations with white employees had been good. Nevertheless, it was commonly believed by other Negroes around town that jobs were not available for them at either place. Opportunities for advancement are limited.

At present two Negroes have full-time jobs with two local construction companies, and during summer vacations additional Negroes are hired. No discrimination is evident, although as elsewhere they do only unskilled and semiskilled work. Aside from white-collar work, a Negro could probably go as high as his interest and ability would take him.

Only one food store has ever hired Negroes. None of the others has sought Negro workers, and if any were used it probably would be only in the most menial and unskilled capacity. The one store employing them said it was always willing to engage them, but none had applied until the summer of 1951, and then only after the writer made known the store's attitude. The girls are holding down regular service jobs. Relations between white and Negro employees are good.

Now what of those businesses in which Negroes have not been employed, at least in recent years? These can be divided into two categories. The first includes places where they might get jobs—for example, the local movie theater. No Negro has ever worked or applied for a job there, but at least one attempt was made by management to employ a Negro. An official said he "was so impressed by George

Dobbs that I tried to get him [in 1950] as one of the ushers, but he had a better paying job and wouldn't take it" (WI-87). Should Negroes of this caliber try to work there, they would probably be hired, although they would again be limited to the lower type of job such as ushers and cleaners. The one or two white-collar jobs would be barred to them. The same situation would also hold true for the Pattern Works and for the drug stores, as judged by interview responses. A Negro would probably be accepted for dirty and heavy labor at the former and a popular boy like Dobbs as counter boy at the latter. Beyond this they could not go.

Negroes have worked occasionally for garages and automobile repair shops, although none has a job in such businesses today. Most such places are probably willing to use them as mechanics and grease monkeys. In addition, Negroes have worked at one period or another in a number of restaurants. Discrimination in all of them is the rule. Many do not hire Negroes except as janitors. In others they are restricted to jobs out of sight of the public, such as dishwashers, cooks, bakers, etc. In no instances do Negroes work as waiters or waitresses. The same is generally true for tourist cabins and hotels. The former have never employed Negroes save in menial capacities and that infrequently. The latter employ them now in this same type of job, most being Southern Negroes working only during summers at the Powahatan Hotel. It is unlikely that more or better such jobs would be available for them in the near future.

The second job category involves those businesses where it is unlikely Negroes will be hired in the foreseeable future. The outstanding example of this policy is the town's second largest employer, the Wire Mill. This firm will not hire Negroes and has not done so since 1935, a sizable number of applicants having been turned down since then. While the leading official of the firm was evasive on this point, another officer was slightly more candid. Although he claimed that all Negro applicants of the last twenty years had either been unqualified or unwilling to accept the job offered, he also stated, "Of course, if I were in his [the personnel manager's] shoes, I would consult management before hiring any colored" (WI-93). Likewise, no Negroes work today at the Toy Factory, probably because of discriminatory hiring policies.

The three public utilities, as well as the town's two banks, have never employed Negroes. No Negro has applied for jobs at any of these places, and it is doubtful that he would be accepted if he did, except possibly in janitorial capacities. As a director of one of the banks said, "'The bank would not refuse a qualified colored girl a job, but would simply shoo her away. She'd never get the job. The other help would probably object, and the directors would just say 'get another white girl' " (WI-66).

The remaining businesses in town do not hire Negroes, even in the usual menial capacities. These include not only bars and taverns, and stores such as furniture, clothing, department, hardware, electric, and five-and-ten cent, but also the professional offices of law, medicine, and dentistry. "Customer reaction" is the usual reason given for these discriminatory practices. It seems unlikely from talks with responsible white informants that Negroes could be hired for most of these positions within the near future, even for janitorial positions. And the Negroes seem to realize these facts, for scarcely any applications have been made.

It should be noted that in this discussion of jobs those associated in any way with either the educational or political areas of behavior have been omitted. These will be covered under their respective headings.

This, then, is the job pattern of Connecticut Town as it affects Negro employment. Drawing it together in more compact fashion, sketching the broad rather than the specific outlines, we note several facts. First, Negroes frequently can obtain unskilled, and in certain instances semiskilled, jobs without too much difficulty. Some firms like the Iron Foundry obviously offer greater chances for improvement and advancement than others. Secondly, almost without exception, no white-collar jobs are open to Negroes. This situation is likely to continue so long as Negro white-collar workers abstain from applying for such jobs, and perhaps even then for some time. Thirdly, most Negro women are in domestic service, and will continue to be so for a long time. This situation owes as much to high school policies which ignore Negro girls for job recommendations and training as to actual discrimination. Fourthly, where Negroes have been employed, they have been held back almost as much by lack of interest, ability, and responsibility as by discriminatory practices. The entire situation was well summarized by a local minister when he said, "You ask me about job discrimination here. Do you see any Negroes working in stores on High Street outside of the Market Basket, and more than that, do you see any hired by the Wire Mill? Also, the Foundry hires no colored women, and no businesses in town have Negroes in any of their offices" (WI-77).

In conclusion, mention should be made of the effect of the Connecticut law against job discrimination on account of race,[8] etc. It can be summed up in the words of a bank director, "The F.E.P.A. would be of no help to [any Negro applying for a job]. It has no teeth in it" (WI-66). Certainly, according to all the informants it has never been appealed to nor used in any case of job discrimination. As one Negro worker put it, "We don't have the time, the education, or prestige to even consider appealing to it" (NI-5). This fact is undoubtedly sensed by the whites. Thus the Act has played no obvious part in the determination and establishment of their policies.

Schools

If there is any institution or area of behavior in Connecticut Town without discrimination, it is the school system. All school facilities are shared equally, and when athletic trips are taken by teams the members live and sleep together without the question of race ever arising.

With respect to student interrelationships on the high school level, the Negroes are generally accorded by their white schoolmates (contrary to the situation in many other Northern schools) the same degree of respect, honor, and friendliness that is given to white students.[9] There are many interracial "best friend" relationships among the boys. Negroes have held virtually every position of honor in the schools. They have been captains of football and basketball teams, class presidents in Junior and Senior years, homeroom presidents, and so forth.

Only two complaints against white students are heard, and these infrequently. The first is name-calling which is generally admitted, even by those who mention it, to be "infrequent and usually by accident" (NI-68). It exists mainly, though not exclusively, below the high school level.

The second complaint concerns the prestige posts which Negroes have never held, e.g., cheerleaders and majorettes. Both apply only to girls. There is some question whether this is due to discrimination. If so, the fault is attributed mainly to the girls' athletic director rather than to the girls themselves. But since these positions are among the most highly competitive in the school as far as girls are concerned, it is possible that the one Negro girl who tried out was not sufficiently talented. This is her own explanation and belief.

As for student social activities, they go to the same dances and while mixed dancing may not be common, it certainly is not exceptional. Moreover, it is on the increase, partly due to the introduction of dancing classes into the school curriculum in 1950-1951. Negro boys took to these more quickly and readily than Negro girls. From what some Negro informants said, the girls are very sensitive to being regarded as too forward or pushy. By contrast, white girls were said by informants of both races to have reacted most favorably, and many asked their Negro friends to have certain Negro boys dance with them.

At the 1950 Junior Prom the May Queen was crowned as usual by the President of the Junior Class, a Negro. Popular Negro boys exchange photographs with white girl classmates as do the other students. Again this is not the case with Negro girls and white boys. Both races go to the same picnics and to many, though not all, of the private parties. About the only thing which has not yet occurred on a high school level is mixed dating, and even this statement must be qualified.*

In the elementary grades discrimination is likewise generally lacking. As suggested by a few white and Negro informants, that which exists is largely because many white children have never before encountered Negroes, and their remarks reflect curiosity and ignorance rather than prejudice.

Student-teacher relationships across racial lines are also generally good.[10] Most Negro children had no complaints to make, and those who had, directed them at only one or two individuals. Thus the girls' athletic director, as mentioned earlier, was felt to be prejudiced by some Negroes. One or two other teachers were also accused of discrimination in class for not permitting Negro students to recite, or for making "occasional slurs on colored people like 'You'll end up at the Foundry anyway,'[11] or for having colored children read in class about the Negro's part in American history which is usually not very complimentary" (NI-60, 61). None of the children, however, claimed that

*See p. 61.

these alleged acts resulted in unfair marking. If not untrue, they are probably exaggerations.

Negro students have won the American Legion essay and oratorical awards as well as the annual award given by the Daughters of the American Revolution to the outstanding member of the senior class.[12] In 1948 a Negro girl was given a scholarship to the Central City State Teachers' College by the local Teachers League. The fact that some of the teachers, including the Superintendent, are southern-born and reared has had no noticeable effect.

Nor is discrimination present in the Parent Teacher Association (PTA). However, Negroes have never been members of it and a few mothers have only occasionally attended its meetings, socials, and suppers. They go as a rule when accompanied by one or more of their Negro friends. Those who have attended were always well received.

No Negro teachers had been hired up to 1952, and there had been only one applicant, a nonlocal woman from New Britain Teachers' College. She was refused a position allegedly because of extreme left-wing political views:

"I asked her what she thought of the United States being in Korea and the general world situation. When she stated that she thought we were overly aggressive and territorially ambitious, I promptly refused to hire her. If it hadn't been for that one thing, I certainly would have done so" (WI-49).

At the time the study was completed the writer was firmly convinced that this statement should be accepted with great reservation. The informant is a native of a border state, is widely known among the white population for his anti-Negro attitude and derogatory stories about them, and plays a key role in the selection of teachers. This writer thus thought it most unlikely that any colored teachers would be hired in the foreseeable future, even if local people favored it. However, error must be confessed here, for in 1953 a Negro woman teacher was hired and assigned to one of the most exclusive elementary schools in the Apple Valley area. To date she has been well received and there has been no hint of any trouble.

Social and Religious Activities

A discussion of religious activities must start from the fact that practically no local Negroes are members of a white church.[13] Most belong to St. Andrews A.M.E. Zion Church; the rest attend churches in Central City if they go at all. Furthermore, with the exception of those who go to the Roman Catholic Church and the Rocky Ledge Congregational Church, none of them attends a white church save for special occasions such as the World Day of Prayer and Thanksgiving services. Such events are managed by the local Council of Churches.

The Council of Churches includes representatives from all Protestant churches, including St. Andrews: the minister, four laymen, and a youth representative from each. There is little discrimination in either the Adult or Youth sections. For the special joint services people seat themselves where they wish, and turns are taken in such responsibilities as collecting the offerings. There is, nevertheless, a certain aura of paternalism about the whole affair. For example, strenuous efforts are made to treat the Negro minister equally and fairly, both in private meetings of the Council and in its public activities. He always has a part to play in all public events, which would not be the case if he took his turn with the other four ministers. It gives the impression of his being continually forced into the public eye. This is often to his detriment as he is not a well-educated man.

In the Youth section a Negro boy was elected chairman in 1950, but this does not mean relations between the two races are without strain. Events such as suppers and dances have a forced atmosphere. Mixed dancing is usually the exception unless one of the ministers takes charge and starts the evening with a Paul Jones type of dance. However, the stress and lack of easy feeling is disappearing with time.

The council's other major activity is the summer Vacation Bible School. It is open to all children without discrimination, and Negroes attend and participate equally with whites. They seem to feel at home and to have no feelings of being unwanted.

On an individual church basis, if Negroes tried to join any of these churches there would probably be resistance by some members although any well-known and respected Negro most likely would be admitted. Once in, most men's clubs would be open to them even though they would not be accepted as social equals. This ought not to be unexpected in view of the middle- and upper-class composition of the Protestant churches as opposed to the lower-class Negro status. The women's clubs would be more hostile, and it is doubtful if many would take Negro members. For both types of clubs, were Negroes admitted it would be on a paternalistic basis at best. The result of the knowledge of this probable type of treatment is to keep the colored out of the white churches except on special occasions, and to perpetuate a racially segregated church. Negro attitudes and the general situation are well described in these remarks:

"Since the churches are largely social clubs, you naturally run into some sort of discrimination. Of course, the services don't have any, but the socials and suppers I went to definitely did" (NI-42).

"I and one or two of my friends went to the Lutheran Church once. No one spoke to me or my friends except Revs. King and Xavier, and we spent the whole time with them" (NI-21).

"We don't like to go as representatives of the colored, but we want to participate in church activities and you can't 'cause you're colored" (NI-62, 63).

As noted the only Protestant Church to avoid discriminatory attitudes and practices is the Rocky Ledge Congregational Church. The two Negro families in Rocky Ledge attend it quite often and participate in many of its activities. As one of the Negro fathers said:

"We go to the Rocky Ledge Congregational Church. They treat us very fine. We're not members of the Church, of course, but they call us members and have us on their waiting [mailing] list. We go to services, social meetings, and Sunday School, and are always made to feel right at home" (NI-64).

His children engage in all the church's youth activities, including its Boy Scout troop; they are just about the only Negroes in town who are Scouts. But these Negro children are the outstanding children of the church. They are recognized as leaders by all the others, and are accepted by them as equals.

The Roman Catholic Church probably is equally non-discriminatory.[14] Those few Negroes who are Roman Catholics and who attend do so fairly frequently and are received the same as everyone else. Any can join and participate who wish, and all church organizations are open to them. None, however, has taken advantage of these opportunities. One favorable factor in this church may be that most local Roman Catholics, like Negroes, are found in the laboring class rather than among management or white-collar workers. The situation has also been helped by having a Negro priest say Mass occasionally. Lastly one must not overlook the authoritarian nature of the Church which makes liberal policies easier to introduce and enforce.

Finally, the Protestant cemetery, but not the Roman Catholic one, seems to discriminate by burying Negroes in one or two sections, and then "People are buried so close to one another and right on top of one another, that it's hard to tell where one person is as opposed to another" (NI-46, 47).

However, this may be due to lack of Negro finances for the buying of plots, or to failure to be sufficiently forehanded about it.

Turning now to nonchurch social activities, relations between children are quite different from those just described, and take place in school for the most part. How much they occur out of school depends on where the Negro children live. Here we can see the effect of a "segregated" housing pattern on social relationships.[15] Negro children living in the "segregated" area usually have few white friends, and they become fewer as the children grow up and organized social activities commence. Under such circumstances, Negroes seldom visit white homes, and whites almost never visit Negro homes. This is especially true for Negro girls. For both sexes friends are chosen from within their environment, from within their neighborhood, and from among the children of their parents' friends. Negro children thus often tend to feel uncomfortable among whites and reject such overtures as are made to them, as for example, invitations to parties. These points are seen in two quotations by Negro youngsters:

"Most of my friends are Negro. This is 'cause they live nearby and also 'cause I feel more at ease around them, can relax, say what I want. Most of their parents, too, are friends of my parents" (NI-75).

"I think the gap between white and colored kids arises on the social level. None of my best or close friends were ever white. I didn't try for them; I didn't reject them. I just picked those I could grab-ass with and not have them talking about me behind my back. As a result, my best friends were Negro boys in this neighborhood. A line has to be drawn at some level between the races, and so I choose Negro friends where there's no line to be drawn. Due to this social gap, I never participated in any school social activities such as dances or parties, but always happened to be out of town or doing something else when they came along. If I'd gone to any of them, I'd have felt funny" (NI-42).

For Negro children living near whites, the social situation is quite different. They see much more of each other, visit more often and intimately, and approach the whole problem differently. They have more chance to participate in the community's social activities, and have "more chance to live a more fully rounded life" (NI-37). There is even, on occasion, mixed dating among children in their early teens. One girl in such a situation described well some of the advantages and disadvantages:

"Most of my friends are white. This is 'cause they live near me and also 'cause there are few colored children my age. Some of those who are my age, my mother and I don't like. I do feel this is sort of a handicap because when all the colored get together, I feel sort of left out, but I wouldn't drop any white friends in order to have more colored. My two best friends [white] live nearby, and we play together all the time, go to each other's homes, eat meals there, eat at Sammy's, etc. Of the boys I like best, two are white. I met them through school, and a bunch of us used to go bowling all the time. There was never any question of embarrassment about being mixed groups. I do think, however, that some of the colored aren't asked to nonschool parties" (NI-76).

Little reference is made by Negroes to either the Boy Scouts or Girl Scouts, and there are no active troops of either for Negro children. Previous Negro troops have disbanded, and no interest has been shown in getting them reorganized. However, where Negroes are members of white churches, as is the case with the Rocky Ledge Congregational Church, they belong to that troop. In any case, neither organization is regarded as segregated by Negro children[16] or parents, and several children belong to white troops.

In those town sports where children compete as individuals, there is no discrimination. Interested Negro children participate equally with others. In the Little League Baseball for young boys, for example, there is complete acceptance of Negro children, and one of the coaches is a Negro. The same lack of discrimination also applies to the American Legion Baseball Club and to the town's Community House which exists mainly for the children's nonschool hours.

The only other nonschool organization to which many Negro boys and young men belong is the Booker T. Washington Club, an all-Negro athletic group. As with the Girl Scouts and Boy Scouts, it too is segregated because of Negro desires but is not regarded by them as being segregated because *they* organized it and did not have it forced upon them. It is active in the town's baseball league, and all Negroes who play ball do so with this club. Before 1952, however, one of the Negro men living in Rocky Ledge played on that area's white team. He left because he felt he was being gradually "frozen out."

There is one children's musical organization, the Junior Musical Society. It is open to colored children although only two have ever joined. One of these was president in 1951; the other is a boy from Foote's Island, just outside of town.

Social contacts between adults of the two races exist almost exclusively on the level of superficial neighborhood or job contacts. Only in exceptional cases do the races fraternize with each other, and when this happens it is generally the whites who make the first move.

On a more organized level,[17] the adults have three musical groups, the Senior Musical Society, the Andante Club, and the Town Band. No Negroes have tried to join either of the first two. It is doubtful if they would be accepted in the first as it consists exclusively of middle-aged and elderly women who are quite prejudiced. As for the second, there would probably not be too much difficulty since it consists of less prejudiced younger people in their twenties and thirties. The Town Band has a Negro member who joined in 1951. He is the only one who has tried to do so recently outside of his daughter who was rejected because she did not have an instrument.

There is no discrimination in the Rotary Club or Chamber of Commerce. The first has no Negro members, although one from the Central City club often comes to town to make up his absences. He is well-liked and respected, and a qualified local Negro, were there one, could probably join. The local Negro minister is a member of the Chamber; doubtless he was admitted because of his race and not because of his qualifications. Due to financial straits and his own feeling of being out of place, he seldom attends meetings.

There is some doubt about a Negro being admitted to the other service clubs. Were the man a known and respected person, he might be accepted on a paternalistic basis although the decision would be far from unanimous. An additional way of judging the clubs is by the fact that one of them gave its 1952 award for good citizenship to the Negro minister.

No Negroes could join any of the fraternal organizations, such as the Masons, the Redmen, or the Grange. In the case of the first two, they would be restricted by race clauses in the charters. A typical answer was, "A Negro join the Masons? No, never, anywhere! Negroes are considered clandestine, and are absolutely barred. No Negro could ever join a white lodge" (WI-72). This bar might not apply to De Molay, the Masonic youth organization, although no definite statement or ruling could be found on this. As for the Grange, a required unanimous vote would take care of any Negro applicants.

Of the town's four veterans organizations, the American Legion, the Disabled American Veterans, the Veterans of

Foreign Wars, and the Veterans of World War II, the first three are open to Negroes. None has any Negro members at present, although the Legion, as has been noted, did have one of Portuguese extraction until 1946 when he died. In 1950 the Legion "supported a Central City Negro by the name of Coleman, head of an all-Negro chapter, for district commander" (WI-36). What this proves is uncertain, and in none of these groups would a Negro find a hospitable social atmosphere.[18] As for the Veterans of World War II, it is doubtful if a Negro could join since it is solely a social organization.

The town's three nationality clubs are the Italian-American Club, the Florentine Society, and the Swedish Lodge. Neither of the first two would admit a Negro, regardless of Italian parentage. One of the members said, "In some chapters, Sicilians are also excluded" (WI-84). For the Swedish club a Negro with Swedish parentage would have to overcome the hurdle of a unanimous vote.

In the realm of private clubs are the Apple Valley Country Club, the Yacht Club, and the Gun Club. The first is the most exclusive social group in town, and admittance of Negroes is out of the question. It is even difficult for Italians and most Jews to get in. The Yacht Club might admit an outstanding Negro, though even that is doubtful. As for the Gun Club, membership is limited only by the long waiting list. Once that difficulty was overcome, there probably would be nothing to keep anyone out.

Three women's clubs, the Green Thumb Club, the Weekly Reading Club, and the Grand Army of the Republic's Woman's Relief Corps, are absolutely barred to Negro women. As the member of two of them put it, "No Negro could get in even if Hell froze over" (WI-104). One other woman's club, the Roman Canasta Association, is largely made up of lower- or middle-class women. While prejudice exists there as elsewhere, Negro women have occasionally participated as guests with no worse result than being ignored by some members. A popular and respected Negro woman might be admitted.

Apart from social activities, but still related to them, are two charitable organizations, the Red Cross and the Visiting Nurse Association. Negroes have played almost no part in either save as recipients of aid.[19] They have given blood to the Red Cross, most of them being unaware, as one of its recent chairmen put it, that "during the war there was a good bit of antagonism to accepting Negro blood or plasma" (WI-98). Only one Negro has ever participated to a greater extent than this. She is the domestic servant of a socially prominent family and served on the Canteen Committee during World War II. She was well treated though with a good bit of paternalism or condescension as would probably be true of any servant. However, she did take her turn serving as chairman of the committee. No other Negroes have volunteered or been solicited.

The Visiting Nurse Association has not even had this amount of participation. It is doubtful if Negroes would be welcome in any capacity save possibly as nurses. However, as with the Red Cross, they have been helped frequently and there is no discrimination against them in the rendering of the services.

Politics

Fire Department policies toward Negroes vary from one volunteer company to another since they are also social organizations, and one is first admitted as a social member. Most companies would probably reject Negro applicants although the procedures would differ. Negroes in the past have been invited to join one or two of the companies with predominantly Slavic and Irish memberships, but refused to do so. If a Negro should seek admittance to these companies today, he would probably be admitted if he were widely known and respected.

The Police Department has two divisions, the regular force and the supernumeraries. Outstanding Negroes might be able to join the latter though it is unlikely that they could make the former.[20] In either case "any Negro who tries has to be better than good" (WI-66), and the ultimate decision is up to the Police Commissioners. As political appointees, they would be greatly influenced by public opinion. In many instances it would be violently against such a move. Said one opponent of Negro membership on the force, "All heck would split wide open if a Negro tried to join. How would you like to go uptown and find yourself looking at some big black cop?" (WI-26). Other factors militating against acceptance of Negroes in either department would be the small number of them in the town, and the still smaller number in the right age bracket who could successfully qualify. Moreover, they have shown no interest in either department and have no tradition of participation.

Negroes receive equal treatment in the courts, and their crime rate is low.[21] The police say they have proportionately no more calls in Negro districts than in others. Many whites believe this is primarily due to the influence of the Negro minister since his arrival in 1946. Negroes have also served on occasional Grand Juries but none are presently serving. A former officeholder said that customarily they are used only "in cases involving Negro murders and other crimes" (WI-87). As for public assistance, one town official remarked that "Negroes are the lowest percentage of all groups on public assistance, and there is little neglect and drinking"[22] (WI-103).

Negro participation and influence in politics are practically nonexistent. They "have always voted, but nothing more"[23] (NI-40). Only one or two do more than work briefly for either political party, and their activities consist mainly in driving other Negroes to the polls. Negroes have seldom run for political office. On one of the few occasions when one did, in the 1951 Democratic Primary race for Probation Officer, he was defeated. It is possible "that persons [who were] athletes, well-liked and admired, could get either voted in or appointed for different political offices if they desired them" (WI-72). There would, of course, be limits to their possible achievements. There has been only one Negro appointment in the town's political history, the naming of the Negro minister to the Housing Committee in 1950. As previously noted, this move aroused much public opposition and effectively killed the chances of public housing.

With a few exceptions, Negroes have not sought or been given political favors. One had a job in the Post Office in 1950 as a temporary employee; he was the only Negro who had ever worked there. Nobody else has ever tried, and none has ever taken the Civil Service exam which is necessary in order to get a permanent job. Any who did so could go as far as he was capable. Two Negroes, of Portuguese extraction, have got jobs from the town government. One worked on the road gang from time to time, and the other held the town garbage collection contract for some years. He was underbid in 1951, however, and lost it.

This general abstinence from politics does not seem due to prejudice, which has had little chance to operate. Rather it can be attributed to the Negroes' low educational level, lack of interest, small numbers, plus lack of leadership and organization.

Despite Connecticut Town's normal Republican tendency, Negroes are still primarily Democratic, as they have been since the 1930's.[24] This allegiance to the Democratic Party is due mainly to the Party's national policies and issues, for, as mentioned above, they have received few favors from it locally.

No Negroes have ever been members of the Democratic or Republican Town Committees, and it is unlikely that any save the most talented could get in for years to come. There have been Negro members of the Republican Club, one before his death in 1950, and one today. Both were active only by comparison with the rest of the Negro community, and then only around election time. Other interested ones could join and might hold office if they had the inclination, ability, and political influence. This is not likely in the foreseeable future. The other political clubs such as the Democratic Club or the Women's Republican Club would also welcome them as members although they would generally be "in the way" on social occasions. Finally, no Negro could possibly join the town's only other political organization, the Apple Valley Political Association. It represents the wealthiest and most exclusive area in town.

Public Facilities

Few public facilities refuse to serve Negroes,[25] although there are certain types of places where discrimination is encountered. As one young Northern-born Negro said, with a fair degree of accuracy:

"All the stores, groceries, and the like are O.K. Any places you go to buy and then leave are O.K. They're glad to have your money. Everyone there is the same, and you don't spend any time in there. But any place you hang around and stay socially, you can feel the tenseness, and you know you're not wanted" (NI-62).

There are, as we shall see, exceptions to this rule. Let us examine briefly each category of facility. The barber and beauty shops, with the exception of one of the former which is operated by a white Portuguese-American in a low-class section of town, do not serve Negroes.[26] This is due to two factors. First, Negroes seldom even consider using white shops, and secondly, the shops have a well-known policy of refusing service. "No barber shops will serve Negroes, and they'll tell them so, too!" (WI-92). As one barber said in freely admitting he does not and would not serve Negroes:

"A couple of niggers came in quite a bit ago and tried to get haircuts, but did I serve them? Hell, no! I have never, and will never, serve a Negro. I won't serve a nigger, and don't want anything to do with them. I'd shut up the shop before I'd serve a nigger. I told the Town Prosecutor one time that he could arrest me if he wanted, but that I'd close up my shop before I'd cut a nigger's hair, and they haven't bothered me since" (WI-16).

Some Negro teen-age boys said they had been to white shops with white friends. They had never tried to get served but had just sat and waited for their friends. All said they had been treated all right, and thought they could have been served if they had wanted to.

Neither of the town's two beauty parlors ever had Negro customers, but one proprietress said, "If a Negro came here for service, I operate a public place, and would do my best to accommodate them if possible. I feel sure, however, that it would hurt my business, but I wouldn't refuse them" (WI-90). Whether this is actually what would happen is open to question.

Discrimination and little Negro patronage are the general rule in the taverns.[27] But there is not a bar in town which has not served a Negro and does not have Negro customers; exceptions are made for individuals whom the managers know and like. Some Negroes and whites claim the situation is improving and that discrimination may have been exaggerated in the past. One Negro who had visited every bar said, "All the taverns are O.K. When I worked at the Iron Foundry I tried all of them on dares. A fellow would say to me that we couldn't use this one or that one, so I'd make a bet and try it. I was never refused service anywhere" (NI-18). However, only three bars operate completely without discrimination; for one of them this is a fairly recent change in policy. As one owner admitted:

"If I had served them before, all my regular customers would have walked out, but today we serve them like everybody else, and usually have one or two a week, always out-of-towners. The local ones got scared off years ago. If they came in today, I'd serve them, but I'm not looking for them" (WI-26).

The situation is somewhat unclear regarding the privately owned public beaches.[28] Many Negroes said they had used Twin Beaches since 1940, although not recently, and had never had any trouble. They knew of no discrimination there. A larger number, most of whom had never been there, said there was discrimination. Some said they would never go there because when they had driven in, they had never seen any other Negroes and had assumed they were not welcome. In any case, since it is slightly off the beaten track, if for no other reason, no Negroes patronized it during the two years of the study.

At the only other beach of this type in the town, the situation is again not quite clear. Negro school children said they had been swimming there recently, both alone and with white friends, and never had any trouble. Still other Negroes said that, when living near there as late as 1940, they had used the beach and had never been bothered. On the other hand, a larger group, none of whom had ever swam there, said Negroes were not welcome and were strictly forbidden from swimming. The owner said, "I don't know as I'd care to have them around the beach if I could shoo them off. I don't want them hanging around. They'd hurt my business" (WI-76). He had, however, no objection to renting them fishing boats. All he wanted was to keep them away from the beach proper, which he said they did.

All other beaches in town are privately owned and operated clubs, not open to the public. Negroes are absolutely barred.

Only one of the clothing and department stores has any discrimination.[29] This is Jones' Department Store. It has had for many years a woman clerk who refused to serve Negroes or to allow them to try clothes on. Even a new management which allegedly disapproves of her attitude has not been able to change it. Nevertheless, most Negroes still shop there, avoiding her if possible, and many do not complain of her attitude. Another store, The Clothes Horse, had the worst reputation for discrimination, but has completely outgrown it since 1951 when there was a change in management.

Only those restaurants combining eating and drinking facilities discriminate.[30] Of the several which fall into this category, the Top of the Hill House, is a high-class, expensive restaurant. One of its managers frankly admitted that most Negroes were not too cordially received although he claimed that it was their lack of cleanliness and presentability which were at fault. Only one or two Negroes interviewed had been there or knew of others who had patronized it; none of them reported any discrimination. As for other restaurants, none of which apparently discriminate, Negroes generally patronize only one or two. This is largely due to their expensiveness although some Negroes imagined there was discrimination.

In the field of overnight accommodations,[31] neither of two tourist cabins investigated had any bar against Negroes as such and both said that large numbers stopped there. One of them had discriminated until about 1949 when they were informed by a Connecticut Civil Rights Commission agent that they would be liable for prosecution if they continued to do so. The only limitations imposed on Negroes are that, where feasible, the owners locate them in the rear of the establishments so as to keep them out of sight as much as possible. It so happens that these are generally the best cabins. Also, one of the operators sets a high standard of dress and appearance for his customers which rules out some Negroes.

Neither of the two hotels investigated had ever had any individual Negro guests or applicants, although Negroes have stayed at one as members of conventions, e.g., the Association of Wives of Congregational Ministers and the State Baptist Convention. The other hotel has Negro parties each year for the benefit of Negro charities in Connecticut Town or Central City. One of its owners said any Negroes wanting to use the facilities would be welcome. Both places claimed that should Negroes of an upper socioeconomic class apply, they would be admitted, but said they had never been approached by such persons. In either case, due to the type of service offered, local Negroes have little need for the facilities and have never used them.

All drug, grocery, and food stores, as well as the various appliance, furniture, radio, electrical, and hardware stores provide equal treatment for Negroes. In solitary instances there were complaints by Negroes of having been kept waiting or passed over in favor of white customers; these and other protests do not appear to be justified.

Both banks give Negro customers equal service as far as processing loans and serving them in turn are concerned. However, as mentioned earlier, one bank has a policy of denying mortgages to Negroes who want to buy into so-called white areas. This is not policy at the other bank, and its officials said all customers were treated on merit. The only unusual treatment allegedly given Negroes by the latter bank is that the manager always inquires as to why money is being withdrawn when accounts are closed out. Although this habit applies to white as well as Negro customers, it sounds like discrimination to people sensitive and aware of discrimination.

Some doctors may discriminate against Negro patients, although most Negro accounts appear grossly exaggerated. The doctor against whom this charge seems most justified is liked, respected, and used by many members of the Negro community. He is accused of refusing to make home calls upon numerous occasions, and one time in particular when he refused to do so the family said they had to deliver a baby. He indignantly denied these charges and said that as far as the baby was concerned, it "had already been born when they called, and it was just a question of the afterbirth. It was all over when they called, and the roads were too bad to justify a trip down." He admitted having refused to make other calls as well, but justified this by saying that "If they can come and save me going to Foote's Island, then they should come" (WI-101). Dentists and lawyers also generally give Negroes equal treatment, and serve them without discrimination.

In the amusement field, the Monte Carlo is the only place for dancing aside from the bars. It is also used for roller skating. Most Negroes were certain they could not dance there and thought the question too silly even to ask. Others disagreed. As for its roller skating facilities, they can be, and have been, used by Negroes. At least two of the Negro informants had skated there.

There is no discrimination at the movie theater on the part of management. However, some Negroes said that whites usually moved their seats rather than sit next to them. Other Negroes denied this; still others said Negroes tended to sit together. It would seem to be a question of how the white individual felt as well as the degree of Negro sensitivity to real or imagined slights.

At the bowling alley there is also no discrimination, and Negroes are welcome. In at least one instance, however, a Negro refused to bowl there, because he did not like the way the white customers looked at him.

In transportation, there is no discrimination. In some cases Negroes were pushed aside by white riders or otherwise insulted, and the bus drivers did nothing to protect or aid them. This attitude of the drivers applies toward members of both races.

Likewise, there is no discrimination in the facilites so far not mentioned, such as garages and dry cleaning establishments. And as for the funeral homes, all white-owned and operated, they appear to give equally satisfactory treatment to all customers regardless of race.

In closing, reference again should be made to the Connecticut F.E.P.A. law, this time with reference to its preventing discrimination in public facilities.[32] Negroes are glad to have it on the books and derive confidence from it; at the same time, none has ever used it or seems likely to do so. Most white informants had only contempt for it as far as its curbing discriminatory practices. Thus, to all intents and purposes, aside from the owner of one hotel who was forced, at a cost of $400, to withdraw the term "selected clientele" from a brochure, and the owner of the tourist cabin mentioned above, it has had little influence.

In conclusion, we can see that the separation of Negroes from whites is most marked in housing, and then, in a decreasing order, in social and religious activities, in the more desirable jobs, in public facilities, politics, and education. Among the other studies with which these findings might be compared are Myrdal's Rank Order of Discriminations in the South[33] and the testing of this order by Banks[34] and Edmunds.[35] Our findings do not agree closely with any of these, possibly because all the studies deal more with attitudes than with actual behavior. Myrdal and Edmunds contrast white and Negro attitudes, and Banks concentrates on the attitudes of Negroes.

Let us summarize briefly each area of behavior. About three-fifths of the Negroes live in the "segregated" area within one or two blocks of the railroad and the major industries. Buying or renting homes for Negroes is practically impossible elsewhere. In addition the Iron Foundry contributes to the segregation pattern through a Negro "colony" of its own. Negro-white neighborhood relations are friendly but involve only limited contacts.

In the social and religious area of behavior we find the only Negro institution paralleling one found in white society, St. Andrews Church and its social clubs. Few Negroes regularly attend any white Protestant church, and Negroes trying to join any of them would encounter some opposition. In church social activities they would be less welcome. The Roman Catholic church has less discrimination, and Negroes would have less difficulty participating in its activities. As for the Council of Churches, it is without discrimination and Negroes participate in all its activities though ignored at its social functions.

Most Negro women work as domestics or as unskilled and semiskilled labor in the Shirt Factory and a few other businesses. Those with more skills or desiring other work almost invariably must go to Central City. Negro men are also limited to unskilled and semiskilled jobs, mainly at the Iron Foundry. Where Negroes are employed, they seem to be treated equally with whites up to and possibly including the supervisory ranks, although certain jobs are not traditionally open to them. Relations between white and Negro workers are generally good though there is little contact between them off the job. The CIO unions, to which most

Negro workers belong, pratice no discrimination. As for the Connecticut F.E.P.A., it has had slight effect in prohibiting job discrimination.

Segregation is present in the public facilities, but varies greatly from one facility to another and has no wholly consistent pattern. On the other hand, in politics there is little discrimination. The lack of Negro participation is due mainly to their lack of interest and ability, and they get equal treatment in all circumstances, e.g., in the courts.

The school system is the "freest" area of behavior for Negroes. Negro children engage in most school activities as readily as white children. Negro-white relations, student to student and student to teacher, are good and improving. Furthermore, social contacts among white and Negro pupils out of school, though limited, are increasing. Segregation is also absent in the PTA though few Negroes belong to it or participate in it. And the situation seems promising for Negro teachers.

Thus, since the race relations pattern is not uniform, it is difficult to be specific in describing the relative statuses of the two races. This is so not only because there are variations from one area of behavior to another, but also because frequently the definition of the Negro's "place" is not clear. Indeed, it is confused by considerations which are at most only indirectly connected with race. The restaurant owner claims that he refuses to serve Negroes because they are "lower class," and the factory management claims, probably with an equal amount of reason, that few Negroes qualify for promotion. Still, segregation exists, and while the outlines of the pattern may be vague, the core of it is solid. Some statuses open to whites are closed to Negroes, and while Negroes may be admitted to others, they are not allowed full participation. The Negro therefore lives in a somewhat separate world: he inhabits certain sections of town; he has his own church social activities; and he is barred from most private clubs and organizations as well as from many public facilities. At the same time he works with whites, although usually on a lower level, and is allowed to participate on an equal basis in the schools.

CHAPTER FOUR

Processes and Techniques of Control

The race situation just described is maintained by a number of factors and processes. These include both impersonal or automatic factors as well as personal or conscious ones, and are reported by both Negroes and whites. There have already been indications of what some of these processes might be. This chapter will be devoted to classifying, describing, and analyzing the processes and techniques of control as they operate in Connecticut Town.

Impersonal Factors

The impersonal factors are those conditions arising out of the social and natural environment which tend to perpetuate the status quo. They are only indirectly related to white or Negro action, and are not immediately or directly imposed by any one group on another group. They can be divided into four categories.

Differences in Socioeconomic Status. These are the first and the most important of the impersonal factors,[1] and to a great extent they are responsible for the present position of the Negro in Connecticut Town. As one of the Negroes' better white friends said, though overstating it, "I don't think there's any discrimination at all against Negroes as Negroes, but only in terms of what they are socially and economically, and of how they behave" (WI-54). Three distinct subfactors go to make up this category. All are interrelated and reinforce each other. They are (1) a low educational level (including a lack of skilled job training) ; (2) a low income; and (3) a low degree of dependability or responsibility. To be sure, discrimination as one factor among many—the heritage of slavery, the original low status of cultural development on the part of Negroes as defined in this New England culture, the relatively short time since emancipation, and the predominantly rural Southern cultural background of the Negroes—accounts for the Negro's comparatively low socioeconomic status in Connecticut Town. At the same time the general race relations situation may also be regarded as partially resulting from the operation of such impersonal forces, and the consequences are such as flow inevitably from such conditions, no matter what racial or ethnic groups are involved. Let us examine each of the above subfactors as it applies to the various areas of behavior, realizing as we do that in many instances it is impossible to separate one from the other and that they necessarily overlap.

The relatively low level of education[2] (thirty-nine of the seventy-eight Negroes interviewed had not gone beyond the ninth grade) is a serious handicap in three areas of behavior: jobs, social and religious activities, and political activities. When combined with lack of necessary training, as is usually the case, it means that most Negroes cannot advance beyond a certain point in jobs. At the Iron Foundry, for example, "The reason for most Negroes not being in certain jobs is that most of them haven't much mechanical aptitude. We have a mechanical aptitude test with a passing mark of seventy-five that we insist upon. None of them, due to lack of education, has ever passed it" (WI-94) .

The same general situation also applies for the unions. As one Negro women said, "I went to one union meeting, but couldn't understand what they were talking about, and I haven't been since. I never know much about anything" (NI-36) .

On a social level, one of the town's leading ladies said, "One of my biggest gripes about the whole problem is that there are so few cultured and respectable Negroes" (WI-57). This barrier, rather than any active discrimination by whites, is one of the main reasons Negroes have never participated in most white social clubs, churches, or organizations such as the PTA, the Red Cross, and the Visiting Nurse Association. Where his low educational level keeps the Negro from certain activities, white prejudices and techniques of control seldom have a chance to operate. This condition was well described by one of the most respected members of the Negro community. "The only whites I've ever met and known at all well have been my employers, but they're a different class from us, and we just don't have the same interests and can't talk easily together. So we just don't bother seeing them" (NI-1).

This barrier is found also between the two races in neighborhood relationships. One young Negro girl said, "We have very fine neighbors. We get along fine, chat with them, borrow from them, and vice versa, but, of course, we never visit each other. We have different social backgrounds and besides we wouldn't feel right" (NI-50).

Finally, the effect of a low educational level can be seen in the almost total abstention of Negroes from politics. Said one Negro, "I don't know enough to even be interested in politics, and if I were, what good would it do me? I don't have enough school to hold any political office" (NI-5). For the same reason Negroes cannot serve in any important capacities in the political clubs or organizations, most of whose members come from the middle or higher socioeconomic brackets of society. The only municipal jobs Negroes could justifiably hold would be on the town's road gang or as garbage collector. As one of the leading politicians stated, "Only one Negro has ever been named to an appointive office, Mr. Beach, who was placed on the Housing Commission. There are no others qualified for such offices, and he isn't even qualified for that one, but we had to have someone representing the Negro point of view" (WI-35).

The Negro's marginal status in the community and his lack of participation in various areas of activity are also explained in large part by his much lower income level.[3] In housing, for example, it limits both renting and buying possibilities. As one of their younger white friends said, "Negroes have the problem of finances. They just don't have the money needed to buy or rent as freely as the ordinary individual" (WI-36).

In the occupational area the Negro often finds himself forced by economic circumstances to take any job he can get, even physically undesirable jobs if they pay enough. The job is valued for its pay, rather than for the nonmonetary satisfaction it affords. The Negro thus exhibits little or no interest in those jobs where the present financial returns are not as great, though they may be more pleasant and hold greater future possibilities. This is the case at the Iron Foundry where Negroes have avoided easier but less lucrative jobs such as painting, plumbing, or carpentry. Said one of them. "I don't think many of them want jobs outside the Foundry because they don't pay enough" (NI-62). This economic pressure and drive also has its indirect effect on Negro participation in union activities since many men find it necessary to hold more than one job. Nine of the twenty-eight male Negro workers interviewed could duplicate this statement: "I don't usually go to union meetings 'cause I work two shifts" (NI-57).

This financial factor likewise operates in the political field. "The only thing that attracts most of the colored is the money they can earn at the Iron Foundry. So the colored here are willing to do only hard foundry work, and aren't interested or capable of participating in other community activities such as politics" (NI-60, 61). Furthermore, they

avoid and show no interest in such jobs as the road gang
or the Police and Fire Departments, again because of the
low pay scale. Still another aspect of this low economic
status may be the alleged buying of the Negro vote.

In social and religious activities, the Negro's economic
position also plays a part, and the same generally holds true
for school social activities. Many Negro children have avoided
such school events as proms "largely because they didn't
have the money" (WI-71); this is also the case with reference
to many public facilities. "I've never been to a restaurant
because I don't have the money" (NI-38).

Finally, there is the subfactor of inadequate responsibility
or dependability.[4] While it may not invariably be linked to
socioeconomic status, it seems to be correlated with it. In
housing it is closely related to the problem of economics, for
it is not always possible to distinguish between financial
inability and plain irresponsibility. The only white realtor
to sell to Negroes said, "I've sold them houses. The big
problem there, however, is that they seem to find it hard to
finance them. They could have built many more if they had
shown evidence of good faith to pay. That's the principal
trouble" (WI-63).

This lack of responsibility bars Negroes from certain jobs,
because employers are less willing to give them a chance.
The Iron Foundry has had many instances of Negro workers being absent or late to work for no valid reasons,
and at least three other employers have had the same experience. Such irresponsibility likewise affects their credit
position in some public facilities, and in some cases people
will deal with them only on a cash basis. As one white doctor
said:

"The type of Negro here in Connecticut Town assumes
no financial responsibility, and so I just don't encourage
them. If a Negro comes in, I treat them the same as anybody
else. I don't draw any lines against them, but I'm more

strict with them. I ask for money on the spot, and I send them no bills. I've had too many sad experiences with them" (WI-91).

This characteristic of irresponsibility helps set the over-all pattern of white thought. It influences attitudes and behavior toward Negroes in all aspects of life and areas of behavior. This is well demonstrated by the remarks of a white lawyer:

"Much of the discrimination is due to the Negroes themselves, though by no means all of it. They're a small minority, and some of them are bad, and they hurt those who aren't. The Greens owe everyone. They get credit and then they don't pay their bills. Or they get drunk and call up asking for loans. Or take Bill Martin. He's just gone into bankruptcy to avoid his creditors. And Sally Cantwell. She's O.K. and means well, but every now and then she finds a bottle of whiskey or a new boy friend, and then she doesn't pay her bills. Or Knight. If you send the sheriff down, he'll pay his bills, but otherwise he just forgets or doesn't understand what it's all about. A very large percentage of them have nonpaying debts" (WI-21).

Nonlocal Background. A second impersonal factor affecting the race relations situation is the largely nonlocal background of Connecticut Town's Negro population.[5] Forty-two of the seventy-eight Negroes interviewed, or 54 percent, came from the South. Thirty-seven of these, or 88 percent are from rural or semirural areas with all that this implies in terms of cultural retardation by New England standards. Another thirteen individuals, or 17 percent, are from still other sections of the country, and five more, or 6 percent, are from foreign countries. If only those over twenty-one years of age are included, the percentage of nonlocal Negroes rises from 77 to 88 percent. In general, therefore, Negroes are regarded as strangers in Connnecticut Town whose residents, like so many others in small New England villages, do not take readily to newcomers. They are handicapped because most of them are late arrivals from different cultural milieus. This picture is further complicated by the rural background mentioned above. The Southern field hand has a difficult time adjusting. His values and social skills are all wrong for New England industry. In this situation even the old and respected Negro resident has found himself lumped with the "rabble" that came in around the time of World War I.

For their part, Negroes do not feel themselves a part of the community in many ways, and so do not participate in its activities as much as they otherwise might. "Many Negroes here, being from the South, aren't really a part of Connecticut Town, and aren't interested in participating in its life more than they do" (NI-40, 41). More specifically, one of the Fire Department officials said, in trying to explain why Negroes had rejected invitations to join, "They haven't been here long enough. The Negro colony is fairly new, and they don't yet feel a part of Connecticut Town. But they will as they live here and raise families, and the next ten years should bring a decided change" (WI-69).

Effect of Numbers. A third impersonal factor is the effect of minority numbers or their rate of increase on majority prejudices and discriminatory actions.[6] Other things being equal, the larger the proportion of a minority in a population, or the higher its rate of increase, the more discrimination there is by the dominant group. While it seems scarcely possible that—with a mere 170 Negroes, or 1.5 to 2 percent of the population—their numbers could help explain the amount of discrimination and segregation found today, the doubling and tripling of the Negro population which took place from 1910 to 1920 and 1930, probably had an important effect. Furthermore, it seems likely that in the future any additional increase in their numbers would affect the

Negro position still more adversely. The only possible exception might be in politics where numbers mean votes.

Housing Shortage. Mention can also be made of one other impersonal factor. This is the over-all housing shortage from which both Connecticut Town and the country at large suffered up to the time of this study. It is in great measure responsible for the Negro's plight in this area of behavior. As a local banker said, "I don't think colored housing is very good here. I feel, however, that it's as much due to the generally poor housing situation as to any outright discrimination. I feel it's part of the entire housing problem" (WI-75) .

White Mores and Rationalizations

Among the more common but less distinguishable processes tending to perpetuate the race relations pattern is the pressure of the mores on the dominant white group. First defined and described by Sumner in *Folkways*,[7] mores are commonly understood as folkways which exert a powerful pressure on individuals to make them conform to what is seen as the proper way to act. In this case the mores are the influence of the white community as a whole upon its individual members to maintain the racial pattern of relationships. This pressure involves the interpretation by each individual of just what each mos* means and how strong it is, regardless of whether his interpretation be correct or incorrect.

Closely related to these mores or to a conflict between different sets of them, e.g., those defining relations with Negroes in contrast to those setting forth religious and political ideals, are white rationalizations.[8] The process of rationalization is a well-known psychological phenomenon,

---

*Mos is the singular of mores.

and meets a powerful human need. A man acts badly and knows that he has deviated from his professed ideals. Still, being under the pressure of the mores defining ethical conduct, he must excuse his actions and protect his status in the eyes of others. Thus rationalizations in this instance operate to give a justification for discrimination or to shift the blame onto others; in either case they ease one's conscience. Let us see how the mores operate to get white conformity, and how the whites then explain and rationalize their actions. In the course of doing this, it is interesting to note that many of the informants are not at all defensive about their attitudes.

In housing almost every white informant who was asked if he would sell or rent to Negroes replied that while he would be perfectly willing to do so or to have his neighbors do so, he would not act without getting the neighbors' prior approval.

"As to selling my home to even a high-type and high-class Negro like Mr. Crawford [a Central City lawyer], I'd be willing to sell as far as I was concerned, but I don't know what I'd do. If it were my cottage, I'd definitely not sell to colored regardless of whom they were, because I know how my neighbors feel and they dislike colored. As for this house, I'd check first with the Irvings and Pearl Muller, because I wouldn't want to do anything to harm them. I'd pay no attention to my other neighbors, however" (WI-95).

"I'd be perfectly glad to sell to a nice Negro family, but since most of my neighbors wouldn't agree with my doing so, I'd have to consider their views if I were to remain here in Connecticut Town" (WI-12).

"I wouldn't sell to a Negro, regardless of who he was or what his socioeconomic status, for business reasons. I'd be ruined" (WI-52).

A more obvious rationalization used in housing is that

Negroes would not be happy living near whites. Two reasons are customarily given for this: the whites would be hostile, and Negroes are just different. These two ideas are well expressed in these quotations:

"I'd feel badly about it if a Negro, even of my own socio-economic class, moved into this neighborhood. I know it's not the Christian attitude to take, but I doubt if I'd take active steps against them such as signing a petition to keep them out, but maybe I'd even do that. If they lived here, they'd be snubbed and wouldn't be happy, and I hate for people not to be happy" (WI-83).

"If any Negroes, no matter how good or fine, moved into this neighborhood, the majority of people would kick about it. As for myself, I'd have to think about it. I feel there's a place for everybody, that it's a free country. However, they're better off by themselves in their own section. That doesn't mean I'd not treat them the same as anybody else. I wouldn't want to do anything to cause them to feel unwanted, but they just have different ways from other people, just like the Jews do, and if one comes in, others always follow. If they have their own sections, there's no discrimination against them" (WI-86).

The housing rationalization that naturally appealed most to the real estate brokers was the old saw that property values would be endangered.[9] Said one such man:

"My real estate company always investigates the prospective client, regardless of his color, nationality, or religion. If, after doing so, we feel that property values would be lowered by selling to him, then we refuse to do so. Naturally, that would always be the case with Negroes" (WI-35).

This rationalization is related to the belief that Negroes are dirty, untidy, and incapable of caring for their property. One white said, "I've only the greatest contempt for the way they live now and keep their property. At present all they do is pull down any neighborhood into which they move. As a result of this, they have a lot of trouble buying and renting" (WI-92). We saw earlier that this is not necessarily the case.

An example of the actual pressure which one's neighbors can bring to bear is seen in the case of a Democratic politician who strongly favored the housing project. Said he, "So many foul and vicious slanders were made against me that I had to call on a number of persons and get apologies under threat of suits" (WI-55).

In the occupational field the pressure of the mores is about as strong. Most informants who were asked if businesses would hire colored employees replied, as did these persons:

"I'm sure Negroes could only get certain jobs uptown in the stores. They couldn't do otherwise in view of the way their customers feel about them" (WI-92).

"All the stores here or anywhere need clerks acceptable to their customers, and if they're prejudiced against certain people, obviously they won't be hired. It would be the same thing if a person had a badly scarred or disfigured face" (WI-93).

The school system also seemed to be in this category as far as hiring Negro teachers. One School Board member said, "I don't know if a Negro teacher could get a job here or not. My personal reaction is that it would make no difference, but I'm not so sure but that if we hired one she wouldn't have two strikes on her to begin with. We have to reckon with the public's prejudice" (WI-94).*

This reply came from many different types of businessmen, too. Generally the reaction to the question was an outright "No," that they could not afford to hire Negroes at all or in certain jobs because of the anticipated customer reaction. Only in one or two instances was a manager professedly willing to try Negro help. Said one such man, "If

*We have seen that this proved not to be the case. See pp. 56-57.

we had a vacancy and a qualified Negro applied, he would be taken in on a trial basis. Then, if everything went all right, and there was not too much customer reaction with too noticeable a drop in local trade, it would be made a permanent appointment" (WI-25). Many people felt this way about hiring Negro policemen or other civil servants.

Some owners and managers referred to the possible reaction of their white employees against working with Negroes as equals. It was argued that if they were not favorably disposed to having Negroes employed in the same place of work and at the same jobs they would walk out or otherwise cause trouble. One bank director said:

"Whether or not we'd hire a qualified Negro for a vacancy would depend first on what the Board of Directors had to say about it, and secondly on what the reaction of the other employees was. If they should protest against the appointment of a Negro, or walk out for example, then we'd of course not be able to hire a Negro" (WI-35).

Some businessmen even claimed that no one, white or colored, was hired without the approval of the rest of the staff. Said one firm's Number Two man, "Hiring Negroes for the office is out of my jurisdiction, and I really don't know. I'd hazard a guess, however, that they'd be greeted with animosity by the other girls. I think it'd be true of almost any office, and therefore they would not be hired" (WI-93). The alleged uncleanliness or diseased condition of Negroes was also often cited, as well as the assertion that they would not be happy or fit in well. The over-all attitude seemed to be that they were in business to make money, not to reform society or be do-gooders.

With respect to the availability of public facilities to Negro patrons, most proprietors worried about the effect of Negro clients on their regular trade. A typical statement was, "I wouldn't serve Negroes in my shop for fear of losing my other customers" (WI-20). Even those who did not themselves discriminate admitted that there was some validity to this rationalization. Said two proprietors who serve Negroes in tourist cabins and a bar respectively:

"The more Negroes are in evidence, the more business is hurt" (WI-41).

"All customers, white and Negro, are given the same service. I don't and never have discriminated against Negroes. Frankly, I think this policy has cost me some business, but not a vital amount" (WI-30).

Some proprietors tried to avoid direct pressure from the mores, not by excluding Negro patrons altogether, but by trying to impose special limitations such as giving them different calling hours. Some taverns, two barber shops, and a dentist and a doctor follow this procedure. Said the dentist, "If I know who they are when they call up, I try to have them come in before noon so that they run into as few whites as possible. But I don't insist upon it" (WI-23). The doctor often takes white patients ahead of Negro ones.

In the social and religious area of behavior, public opinion was consistently assumed to be hostile to Negro participation. It was said, for example, that they would not be happy or at home in these organizations and activities, and that they were unsanitary. The first of these viewpoints is well expressed below:

"If any Negroes tried to join our church, they'd probably feel very much out of place. We'd try and show them that ahead of time, of course" (WI-3).

"In a white church they'd feel out of place, not at home, and not happy. Why, if you took away their church and put them in white churches, they wouldn't run anything, and would be cramped and unhappy. They prefer their own church. Of course, they could go to ours or any other if they wanted, though I'm not so sure about joining. But they wouldn't want to. Being in their own church is the only way they can exercise any initiative at all. After all, they have been only out of the jungle 100 years while the whites have been out for over 2,000 years" (WI-98).

White Techniques

The processes operating to maintain the race relations pattern which have thus far been examined have not been discriminatory per se, or have been so on a broad and diffuse level. We turn now to an examination of deliberate and specific actions by whites against Negroes.

To date these techniques have only been mentioned in passing in race relations literature. There has been no specific or systematic discussion of them, or even an attempt at complete listing. This we will try to do below. The only parallel to this approach is Myrdal's Rank Order of Discriminations.[10] Furthermore, in the general literature on social control such listing as there has been of the techniques of control has been done largely on a direct process level without reference to specific communities, situations, or relationships. Our listing of the control techniques will be done not through any rigid classification, but rather through what might be called a loose order of completeness or intensity. As will be seen, the following quotations largely describe the techniques used and incidentally emphasize the importance of participant observation as a method of discovering them:

"Discrimination is here, but it's more or less under cover until you try to get ahead. It's quite subtle" (NI-50).

"Such discrimination as there is, is done in a shrewd way. Lots isn't open to the eye. You have to live here awhile to see it. They just give you the run-around" (NI-8, 9).

Violence. This is the most radical of all control techniques and includes not only the actual use of it but also the threat of it.[11] Fortunately, other techniques in Connecticut Town are so effective that there has been little call for such extreme measures. The only occasions on which violence has been used have been when Negroes have moved into white neighborhoods. At such times some white children have put their parents' words into action by stoning or fighting Negro children. These actions have never lasted very long and have never succeeded in forcing any Negroes to leave areas they had entered. However, a few Negro families have rejected opportunities to live in white neighborhoods for fear such violence, or worse, would occur. One couple remarked, "You have to be awful careful about things like that. It might be like Chicago or Cicero. I'd hate to have them burn my house down" (NI-62, 63). Even where the Negroes do not fear actual violence, the reaction of whites can be very extreme and unfriendly.

Direct Refusal and Insult. These two techniques[12] operate in the context of direct white and Negro contact, and are found in four areas of behavior. However, direct refusal and insult are not among the more commonly used methods. This might be due to the fact that they are frank and unequivocal, placing responsibility solely on the person using them. He is thus forced to face the problem squarely, without excuses or rationalizations to ease his guilt feelings. This was the theme of Myrdal's *American Dilemma.*[13]

This over-all technique is a serious impediment, despite its general lack of use, to the improvement of Negro housing. Generally speaking, outright verbal refusal and insult is used by real estate men and by individuals selling or renting their own homes. The former are less important in terms of the volume of Negro purchases. As a leading politician said, "No real estate firms in town will handle any Negro business" (WI-55). Approached by few Negroes, most firms would probably refuse to serve them, or if they did so it would be only in unpopulated or nonwhite areas.

Negroes trying to buy or rent almost invariably work through individuals. The pattern here is much the same, outright refusal. "People won't sell to them" (WI-78). This applies not only to homes, but even to garages.

"You know that little house of Goens' behind the High School? My sister asked if we could rent it, but he said he wouldn't rent to colored. And there have been other cases like that, too. They just won't rent to you. I inquired myself at one place behind the post office which was for rent, and the man said he didn't rent to colored. He was nice about it. He said, 'I'm sorry, but I don't rent to colored.' I thanked him and left" (NI-48, 49).

"I tried all of Goens' houses, two of them on Powahatan and Seaview Streets, and he told me he would rather see them collapse than rent to Negroes" (NI-62).

"Whites won't even rent garages to you here in Connecticut Town. I tried to get one from a fellow up the street, and he wouldn't even consider it. He just kept saying, 'No, no!' " (NI-29).

Or the insult aspect of the technique may be used after Negroes have moved into a neighborhood where whites do not want them, in an attempt to get them out. This is seen here:

"Neighbors can be pretty nasty if they don't want you. When we first lived here, the nearest neighbor put up string to keep us off their property. It couldn't have been more effective if it had been a stone wall. Some of the others weren't nice at first either, used to yell at us and call us names. Mrs. Hart said the same thing happened to her at first" (NI-58).

This technique is used infrequently to deny Negroes jobs. For example, the Iron Foundry uses it against Negro women and the Wire Mill against all Negroes. As one of the white officers in the USW at the Iron Foundry stated, "I recall one woman who applied and was told frankly by the Foundry that they didn't care to get into the problem of hiring colored women" (WI-84). In another case involving the same company the owner said that "the place for Negro women was in the kitchen, not in the shop" (NI-62).

Insults are found in the schools, too, in spite of the over-all lack of discrimination there. They might almost be discounted, however, since according to most Negro inform-ants, they are usually done accidentally and not with the intent to keep the Negro students "in their place." They consist largely of name-calling by white students and seem to occur only in anger or forgetfulness. This happens mostly on the grade-school levels. Allied to this practice is the tendency by some white children to make coarse remarks about Negroes whenever they see them in films, particularly in ones like the *Home of the Brave* which deal with the race problem.

Teachers apparently use this technique occasionally, again on a largely unconscious level. On one occasion, for example, "Our Glee Club teacher had us sing songs derogatory of Negroes. We went up to her afterwards and protested, but she just said that the rest of the girls didn't mind and refused to do anything about it" (NI-50). It is also seen from time to time in slurs made against colored children. The probable effect of such attitudes and remarks is not to force Negro children to withdraw from school and other activities, but rather gradually to create in their minds the idea that they are different—and inferior. Thus a frame-work for later discriminatory techniques is established.

The most frequent and best known examples of this type of control are found in certain of the public facilities, particularly the bars and taverns. One bartender spoke frankly when he said, "There are lots of ways you can get around them: put a head on their beer, serve them in a different glass to show you don't want them around, break the glass when they're finished" (WI-19). Or they may be told before being served that they have had enough to drink.

"We went in the Old Hickory and right off the bartender says, 'You've had enough.' I said, 'Hell, I just got here.' but he just repeated himself and waved us out" (NI-16). On at least one occasion a restaurant operator "roughed up Negro customers, pushing them around, and letting them know they weren't wanted" (WI-36).

It is also used in barber shops. Said a white barber, "I've never served a Negro. I've had one or two of them try me and I've always told them I wouldn't serve them" (WI-16). A Negro man remarked:

"When I first came here I tried a barber shop in the Fourth Ward, one on the first floor 'cause I figured all second floor shops would be clip joints. They said they didn't serve colored. So I tried another shop in the main part of town, and they said the same thing" (NI-14).

Economic Pressure. This technique[14] and the two that follow generally fall into the category of institutional devices. In all three instances prior white consensus exists as to what should be done to defend the race relations pattern. Economic pressure operates on two levels. One is actual pressure applied; the other is the fear or threat of it. For example, Negroes trying to buy into white areas often find the selling price has been unexpectedly raised from its original quotation. These statements, by a Negro and a white respectively, describe the technique:

"We had trouble finding a place of our own to buy or to build. In the first place, they put the prices so high. Yes, I personally feel they jack them for 'undesirable' tenants, whether white or colored, though I couldn't prove it. It's sort of invisible and hard to pin down" (NI-60).

"I would refuse to sell to any Negro, regardless of whom they were, who approached me about a house. Even if it was someone like Bunche or [Marion] Anderson, I wouldn't sell to them, but instead of refusing outright, I'd jump the price on them" (WI-50).

Another example of economic pressure applied to prospective Negro purchasers in white areas is the withholding of mortgages by banks, so that Negroes are unable to finance the purchase of a home. In at least one instance, other banks in the metropolitan area were requested to withhold mortgages from certain individuals, too. An example of this is seen below:

"The Carters wanted to buy an old house on Route 11. It was located near the Bottling Company. The owner was willing to sell to them, but the bank which held the mortgage said that if it was sold they would call the mortgage immediately. They even went to the extent, too, of getting other banks here and in Central City to also refuse mortgages" (WI-55).

The Negro did not get the house.

Legalistic Mechanisms. A few of these include constitutions, membership restrictions, and either unanimous or majority votes.[15] They are used by groups of property owners, social and religious groups, and some political organizations. The following quotes give a clear picture where constitutions and membership restrictions are involved:

"The Connecticut Shore Realty Company [a landholding company which gives long-term leases] was expressly formed to keep Negroes and other undesirables out. As things stand and work, the company has to approve and pass on all tenants. If a Negro applied, the request would simply be denied. He wouldn't have a chance. All subleases and mortgages have to be approved by the company, too" (WI-92).

"Where I live, Hilltop Road, is a restricted area, and property is only offered to a selective few. If a person moves from there, the Hilltop Real Estate Company has to have first offer at the property" (WI-93).

"No Negro could possibly be admitted to the Masons or

the Redmen. Definitely not. It's prohibited in the rules of the charter" (WI-35) .

"As for admitting Negroes to the Garden or Reading Clubs, the State Federation of Women's Clubs, to which both belong, specifies that all members have to be white women, and so Negroes could naturally not be admitted" (WI-50) .

In some cases, such as those involving property transactions, the restrictions just described have not been legally enforceable since the Supreme Court's 1948 decision on this issue. Even in 1960, however, this fact is not generally known; when it is, people cling to the old practice in the hope it will scare off "undesirables." To the degree that a hostile atmosphere is created which most people are unwilling or financially unable to penetrate by a court fight, it is, of course, successful.

The unanimous or majority vote systems for excluding "undesirables" are most often used among social clubs and certain of the volunteer Fire Department companies which have an important social function. These devices operate either in terms of the entire membership or of an admissions or nominating committee. The unanimous vote requirement is illustrated below:

"You have to be examined and seconded [for the Apple Valley Country Club] and then the Acceptance Committee has to hand down a unanimous decision" (WI-93) .

"The Fire Department has a blackball [unanimous] system that would make it hard for any Negro to join" (WI-54) .

Majority vote requirements vary from an easy to a stringent policy. A good example of the latter is seen in the procedure followed by one of the service clubs as related by a prominent member:

"When a person is proposed for membership, his name goes first to the membership committee and then before the

board of control. This latter group has to vote on him
three times, approving him each time by a two-thirds or
three-fourths majority. So, in effect, you have what amounts
to a blackball system, and I doubt if any Negro would ever
get through" (WI-36).

The requirement of a specified large majority vote by a
committee or board is also used by the Congregational
Church and the Police Commissioners. Usually, however,
a simple majority vote is required of the membership as a
whole, as in the case of the Episcopal and Baptist Churches,
the Chamber of Commerce, the local Gun Club, certain
Fire Department companies, and the Town Meeting. Depending on public opinion, this technique can be as devastat-
ing as either of the preceding two. As a Baptist deacon said,
"If Negroes tried to join the church and had a letter from
another church, they would have to be passed by a majority
vote. If it was known beforehand they were applying, [their
application] would probably be beaten" (WI-71). Another
example of this was seen in the fate of the proposed housing
project which "was flattened by the Town Meeting"
(WI-60).

Most of these measures can be amended whenever the
membership so desires as has happened with some national
fraternities in recent years.[16] This is customarily a long
and harassing process, and there seems little likelihood of its
occurring in Connecticut Town within the foreseeable future.

Paternalism. In this, the last of the institutional-type
devices,[17] the general attitude is well expressed by the remark,
"Things are done for them, and they are helped when they
need help" (WI-99). Of course, other objectives are obtained
than merely helping people, since paternalism facilitates
containment of the Negroes. In housing, paternalism is best
seen in white efforts to establish a segregated Negro area.
As was mentioned earlier, the Iron Foundry has taken the

lead in this movement. This is borne out by the wife of one of the owners:

"For those [Negroes] who have worked at the Foundry for five years or more, we give land if they will build on it. It is given outright. There is no such thing as a ninety-nine year lease. Of course, it is definitely segregated from other areas, and they are given land only in that one spot, around Western Avenue. Of course, the whole scheme is highly paternalistic" (WI-57).

And one of the company's officers said, "Mr. Irving recently discussed the possibility of building more company homes on Western Avenue for the Negroes. This just goes to show how interested he is in their welfare" (WI-94). That all this effort and propaganda has met with some success is seen in the fact that forty-eight of the town's 170 Negroes live in this area, including the families of two young Negro veterans who took advantage of these opportunities and built their own homes there in 1952.

With respect to jobs, paternalism is found at the Iron Foundry, the Printing Company, and the Shirt Factory. Greater leniency in terms of requirements of dependability is shown toward Negro workers, they are given more favors such as loans, and they are usually more assured of jobs in time of unemployment than are whites. Further, when Negroes apply for jobs which have never been open to them, e.g., secretarial positions, some whites try to find them equivalent positions out of town, usually in Central City. Difficult situations are thus avoided. As one Negro woman explained it, "Mr. Trent helps place Negro women in jobs in Central City. I must say I'm a bit suspicious of his motives in doing so, as he is on the board of the Iron Foundry" (NI-19).

Paternalism is very evident in social relations. Many whites call Negroes by their first names, though the practice is not reciprocated, largely because they know them only as servants or menial workers. Some whites also become Negro patrons, lending them money when in need, or bailing them out of jail if that is necessary. As one young Negro said, "I've lots of close white friends. Three of them are Finch, Paine, and Welch. They'll help you out if you ever get in a pinch" (NI-29).

Paternalism is most important and influential in strictly religious activities as is seen in the white support of the Negro church. It consists both of considerable financial backing for St. Andrews, and also in allowing its congregation the occasional use of white church facilities. One of the most thoroughgoing examples of this control technique and its insidiousness in helping to maintain a segregated religious institution is seen in the following remarks of one of the white ministers:

"I want to see Zion Church [St. Andrews] strengthened and perpetuated. So I got Evan Terhune of Central City Divinity to come in for youth work, and got a white person, Irving, to pay for his salary. I didn't want a Negro for the work because in the past the Negro girls have always chased them, and a lot of them became pregnant. The reason for this set-up and my interest are that today the young people are getting away from Mr. and Mrs. Beach. Another reason for getting a white for the job is that they have to live and work with whites, and the more contact they have with them the better. I don't want the Negroes with no church of their own and therefore going to the white churches. I feel they're better off with their own" (WI-102).

Elimination of Prospects. Closely related to the economic pressures mentioned earlier is the situation found only in housing, where whites buy homes themselves in order to eliminate potential Negro customers.[18] This is said to have occurred a few times. In one instance, "A short time ago that house on the other side of Mr. Cotter's went for sale, and the Polish lady next door stepped in and bought it before we even had a chance, so that she wouldn't have any Negroes living next to her" (NI-11).

In another case, in the attempt to keep Negroes out who were buying through an "undisclosed principal," i.e., having a white person buy for them, the whites who eventually got it had to pay twice its original value.

Excuses. This is one of the most widely used and effective control techniques, and is found in all areas of behavior. Excuses are common probably because they come very close to quieting white consciences. At the same time, contrary to rationalizations, one's status is not at stake; they are only convenient tools. It should also be noted that they are often harder for Negroes to accept than outright refusals. Let us look at them, again by areas of behavior.

Excuses are used by whites seeking not to rent or sell homes to Negroes. The most frequent of these is the "No vacancy" one, used both by real estate brokers and by individuals. Many quotations could be given to demonstrate this, but one of the more detailed is the following by a young Negro man:

"There was also a house on Foote's Island Road near Grammar Street which was vacant for six months while they were trying to rent it. I phoned about it and was given a rough idea of the rent and told to come over and have a look at it. Then they asked me who was calling, and when I said, '———', the fellow put his hand half over the phone and yelled into the next room so that I could hear him, 'Hey, Joe, the Foote's Island house is taken, isn't it?' Then he told me he was so sorry, but it had just been rented to someone else. It was vacant for another six months. Then there was another house on High Street in Connecticut Town proper, right next to the Telephone Company. It has since been pulled down. It was vacant for four months. I phoned them, too, and got all the information on it, but as soon as they found out who I was they said it was already taken" (NI-62).

Another popular excuse, more closely related to the pressure of the mores, is that of referring to neighbors' feelings, saying in effect that while one would not mind in the least selling or renting to Negroes, the neighbors' views have to be considered. As one white real estate man said, "I would show him the house and explain the situation" (WI-52). Not all whites are as gentle as he, however, and this technique is often rather closely related to direct refusal and insult. For example:

"When we left 21 Williams Street, we saw that Mr. Harkins was advertising in the papers about an apartment he had to rent on Harding Avenue, and so we called him about it. He was very friendly at first, and very favorable about letting us have one. Finally I said 'There is one thing I want you to know, Mr. Harkins, I am colored.' Well, there wasn't a sound on the other end of the wire, but when I asked if he would still let us have one of the apartments he said, 'Why, no! Why, no! I wouldn't think of it. All the windows would be broken in no time. Why, what would my neighbors think?'" (NI-58).

In addition to these two principal excuses, there are any number of lesser ones, such as the following: that the house "is too close to the center of town to have colored living there" (NI-50); that "'I wouldn't dare have kids that near the High School'" (NI-57, 58); or that "He'd have to see his wife" (NI-20, 21).

Where jobs for Negroes are concerned, there are a number of common excuses. The usual procedure is to tell the Negro that there is no job opening. For example, the Iron Foundry uses this approach where Negro women are concerned. As one of them said, "My mother tried two or three months ago to get a job at the Iron Foundry, and they just told her they didn't have any jobs open. But they've hired white women since then" (NI-50).

Sometimes this technique is used with a slight variation

as when the firm asks the Negro to return in a few days. When he does he is informed that the job has been already filled, or that no opening exists. The Iron Foundry has shifted to this approach in recent years, and it has been used by the Wire Mill and all other employers who do not use Negro labor. Consider these statements:

"The Iron Foundry won't hire colored women. I tried there four or five years ago, and I could give you a list a mile long of others who have tried, too. They gave them a run-around the way they do all colored women. When I tried I went to the employment agency in Central City, which told me there was a job opening in Connecticut Town. I applied, but Mr. Little gave me the run-around, too. He said he'd let me know in a couple of days. When I went back, he said he'd thought some of the men were going in service, but they weren't at that time. The next time I returned, some white woman had the job" (NI-58).

"I first tried to get a job at the Wire Mill. They told me to fill out a form and to come back in two weeks. When I returned, they told me the job was already filled. I was given the run-around and heard afterwards that they didn't hire Negroes" (NI-51).

Another common type of excuse in this area of behavior is appealing to the alleged prejudices of one's white employees or customers. This can be done by just saying "that the white girls would object" (NI-61), or two subthemes can be brought in. One is often used by the Wire Mill as when it tells Negroes who are applying, " 'If we had ten or fifteen colored fellows working here or applying all at once, we'd hire you, but by yourself you just wouldn't get along' " (NI-57). The other is frequently used by the Iron Foundry, and consists in saying, "They can't hire Negro women because they'd need a special ladies' room and shower" (WI-96).

In the cases of jobs at certain public facilities, particularly those involving close contact with customers, the most frequent excuse given is that customers would object. Said the owner of a beauty parlor, "I just couldn't hire a Negro girl to work here due to my customers. I'd just tell her the truth, that I had no objections, but that I was working for my living, and if I hired her I soon wouldn't have any business" (WI-90).

Finally excuses are frequently made that the Negro involved does not have the necessary qualifications. This applies both to promotion and to certain types of work. As one of the more intelligent and responsible young Negroes rightly said:

"I've found job discrimination everywhere I've been. Certainly it exists at the Iron Foundry at certain jobs which are closed to colored. Another thing, they certainly are not upgraded and advanced as are white. It's a lot harder for them to become foremen. It took . . . the first one I know of twenty-five years to make it. They always say they aren't qualified, but that's often just an excuse made up by management" (NI-60).

In the schools the only excuse used to keep Negro teachers out has been that they are not qualified. Thus, as we have seen, when a Negro teacher applied for a job in 1950 she was rejected on the grounds that her political views were subversive.* But as two whites said:

"Considering Goddard's political questioning of the Negro teacher who applied last year, that type of question was none of his business and certainly not justified" (WI-66).

"They would find some excuse [not to hire a Negro teacher] if Goddard had his way" (WI-71).

The same attitude seems to hold for Negro political participation, too, namely that they are not qualified. While there is some truth to this, it is overdone.

*Again see pp. 56-57.

In the social and religious activities one excuse seems to be sufficient to bar Negroes from participating, namely that they would not be happy. This excuse has been used by both the American Legion and the Baptist Church. Take one case involving the Legion:

"Four Negro vets tried to join the Legion, coming in as a group, and were approved for membership by the chapter. However, before they were formally admitted, the Post Commander talked to them and explained that although they were free to join, he didn't think they would ever be completely satisfied being in a white chapter. As a result of his talk, they changed their minds and joined the Negro post in Central City instead" (WI-81).

Excuses are a common method for preventing Negro use of various public facilities, most frequently those having lengthy and personal contacts with customers.[19] Thus bars often rely upon such excuses as being sold out, or barber shops of "just going to shut up shop" (WI-20). Other facilities such as tourist cabins or hotels rely most frequently upon the "No vacancy" excuse. "We were discreet. We told them very politely we were all filled up" (WI-39, 40). And lastly, some doctors at times avoid Negroes by claiming it was too far to their homes, that they were not the family doctor, or that the weather was too bad.

Evasion or Ignoring. This practice[20] is found in every area of behavior, and as in the case of some other techniques operates on two levels, the actual and the imagined. With respect to housing and jobs, it consists mainly in accepting Negro applications without telling them that they will never hear anything further.

Frequently the first thing the Negro knows is that the house has been sold to some white person:

"We tried to get into that red brick house of Goens' in the Fifth Ward, a little beyond Sammy's. He used to rent to colored there, and when we asked him for an apartment he said he was repairing it but would take care of it when he was through. But he never did. As soon as he got the colored out and repaired it, he rented to whites" (NI-20, 21).

"I've tried to rent a home at least three or four times, and have always been rebuffed. I've called dealers, letting them know I was colored, but none of them ever called back again. And once I answered a [newspaper] ad, again making it clear I was colored, but I never heard from them either" (NI-55).

In employment, ignoring or evasion usually involves a Negro asking for a specific job and then being forgotten:

"I've seen four or five girls come in myself [to the Iron Foundry], and they were always turned down. Several of the husbands went to Little about it and complained. After that they always accepted their applications and told them they'd be notified as soon as there was an opening. They must have twenty or thirty applications by now, but although lots of white women have been hired, they still haven't contacted any of the colored women" (NI-62).

In one or two instances evasion verging on paternalism has been practiced, and Negro women have been offered servant jobs instead of those for which they were applying:

"Our daughter once tried to get a job as a clerk in the Five and Ten Cent Store, and the person interviewing her offered her a job as a domestic servant at his home instead" (NI-64, 65).

"The Iron Foundry won't work any colored women. My wife tried to get a job there, and Mr. Irving tried to get her to work in his home doing laundry and so forth instead of in the shop" (NI-37).

For those Negroes who have jobs, as at the Iron Foundry and Shirt Factory, they are seldom considered for promotion. At the Iron Foundry, for example, "On the whole I think they are slower with Negroes in promotions. I know a lot of men who have been qualified and who haven't been promoted. They just passed them over, probably because of their color" (NI-46). That this policy is deliberate is admitted by one of the officers. "In the effort to keep the peace, we haven't encouraged Negroes to enter these and certain other jobs because of the feelings of some of the men or foremen" (WI-94). The same practice occurs in the smaller stores and businesses when looking for help. Negroes are never considered for the jobs. This may be largely an unconscious process. As one owner said, "When I need help, I usually go to someone I know personally or whose family I know and ask if they are interested" (WI-8).

Within the school system ignoring is relatively unimportant as used by teachers, and is mentioned but infrequently. At such times it consists of such alleged acts as this one. "Miss Roberts discriminated. She allowed colored no classroom discussion or participation at all, and she never called on you. However, her marking was fair and O.K." (NI-30). We have, on the other hand, noted previously the manner in which Negro children were overlooked for jobs upon leaving school. Apparently the school system reflects local prejudices and mores to the extent of not submitting Negro girls' names to local businesses seeking office help. As one businessman said, "We've never been given any Negro girls' names" (WI-93).

In the social and religious area of behavior, ignoring might better be termed "freezing out" or "cutting dead." It has already been seen how Negroes, where admitted into church membership, were ignored in the running of the church and its social activities. This also happens on a social level as indicated by one Negro man. "I get along O.K. with the whites at the Iron Foundry. The only trouble is that in the plant and at the shop it's 'Hi, Bill, how are you?' and there is lots of kidding. But if you see them on the street, especially with their wives, they don't even know you" (NI-14). Negro-white neighborhood relations fall into the same pattern. Said one Negro man, "I never talk to my white neighbors, and they never talk to me. If they want to be friends, it's up to them to make the first move" (NI-12).

The same over-all picture may be painted for the various social clubs and other organizations such as the Red Cross and Visiting Nurse Association. Indeed, in view of relationships between the two races elsewhere, it would be unusual if this were not the case. None of the clubs or social organizations, save the VNA* has ever invited a Negro to join or participate, and any Negroes so rash as to try are given the "freezing-out" treatment. Here is a good example of this:

"I used to play with the Rocky Ledge Baseball Team, and there's plenty of discrimination there. As long as the team was winning, no one wanted me to play, but if they were losing they wanted me to help them. And they don't want to socialize with you. If they see you on the street, they don't even know you. All their friendliness at the ball park is just a front. As an individual they don't see you, but as a group you're O.K. It's all a front act" (NI-62).

In politics, save when a "race" spokesman is felt necessary, Negroes are so much on the outside of community activities that again they are never even thought of or remembered. It is as though they did not exist.

Where ignoring is practiced in public facilities, it is so effectively applied that Negroes seldom challenge it. The technique is well summed up here: "Down South they tell you where they want you and don't want you. Here they all act nice, and they discriminate against you quietly and politely, like serving other people ahead of you" (NI-31). As was brought out earlier, the discriminatory bars and

*However, see p. 65.

taverns are the ones that most commonly act this way. "The bars never refuse you service directly. They just ignore you and keep wiping the bar. That happened to me at Mom's and the Old Hickory Tavern and also at the Old Shoppe where I've been once or twice in the evening" (NI-62). It likewise allegedly occurs in one or two of the groceries and doctors' offices as well as occasionally in appliance stores.

Ignorance and Indifference. These factors are just as important as the white techniques described above, for ignorance and indifference serve just as effectively to perpetuate white control.[21] As long as whites can live undisturbed by or unaware of racial inequities, they can be indifferent to them. The situation rarely affects them directly, and they tend to regard Negroes as members of an out-group to whom "white" standards do not apply.

Indifference for what happens to Negroes is seen in housing in the attitude of a white property owner toward his Negro tenants: "When we got this home, Goens owned it. He didn't repair it or clean it up, so we did the necessary work and then sent him the bill for the materials. He said he'd sold it, and we had to pay for everything ourselves" (NI-20, 21). Two other examples of this attitude can be seen in the failure of another white landlord to rebuild or clean up what was left of a house occupied by Negro tenants after it was destroyed by fire, allegedly because "Negroes live there, and they don't care how they live" (WI-78), and in the failure of this same man to provide some of his tenants with any of the ordinary facilities such as running water or toilets. The fate of the proposed municipal housing project is one more indication of this lack of concern. This general attitude is recognized by most Negroes and by only a few whites.

White indifference is also present in other areas of behavior. Many factory officials do not worry about utilizing Negro labor to the fullest extent of its capabilities. And there is complete lack of concern by most whites as to what public facilities are barred to Negroes. In each case, whites help to perpetuate the present racial situation by this attitude.

Although there is little that can be said here about white ignorance of the race relations situation, it is a common factor in helping to maintain the racial pattern. Where people are ignorant of a situation, they are in effect complacent about it, and so contribute to its perpetuation. This can be seen in the statement made at one time or another by nearly every white informant. "I don't know anything about that."

It is, of course, possible to break through these barriers and make the individuals concerned see themselves and their society as they really are. When this happens, reform often takes place. Montclair, New Jersey, with its well-known Self-Survey,[22] is a good case in point. An appraisal of this sort has not yet occurred in Connecticut Town.

Negro Responses

The race relations pattern could not be effectively maintained without reciprocity between white and Negro. The Negro has to cooperate with the white if the system is to be preserved. Thus, in addition to the impersonal factors, the pressure of the mores on whites, and the white techniques, an important role in the maintenance of the segregation pattern is played by the Negroes themselves. Generally speaking, their behavior can be interpreted as reinforcing and accepting the other control processes. It can best be discussed under the broad heading of avoidance.[23]

Avoidance. Basically, this is the Negro attempt to have as little as possible to do with whites, and is part of his effort to stay in his own community and environment. Stronger in some areas of behavior than others, it is at least partially dependent on the degree of development of the Negro community. Where the community is weak, or the individual Negro's ties to it are weak, avoidance tends to take the form of outmigration.[24] This is the most complete type of Negro avoidance. Rather than fighting or giving in to discrimination, some persons leave town entirely, in most cases going to Central City. Actually, there have been very few instances of this being done. More commonly what occurs might be called "segmental migration," that is, the Negro goes out of town, usually to Central City, only for specific things such as a haircut or social and religious activities. In addition, as has been noted, all the Negro white-collar workers migrate daily for work to Central City because no jobs are available for them locally. In either case, all too often the result is that "the best and most talented [Negroes] leave town" (WI-55), and the local race relations pattern remains comparatively undisturbed. The Negro community thus loses at least some of its potential leaders. We will have more to say about this subject later.

Aside from these particularly specific forms of avoidance by local Negroes are its more general manifestations. By and large these consist of a withdrawal by Negroes from participation in one or more institutional areas. This behavior can best be seen if approached from the point of view of the reasons for withdrawing. It will be clear as we proceed that some of the reasons for Negro withdrawal are the direct result of white actions, while other reasons will not fall into this category.

Rebuff and Fear of Rebuff. Rebuff itself is a comparatively uncommon experience. Very few Negroes have tried at some point to get around the segregation pattern, and those who have done so have tried it for the most part in housing and public facilities. In housing, for example:

"I've tried to rent a home at least three or four times,

and have always been rebuffed. Now I've just about stopped trying" (NI-55).

"After you've been slapped in the face a couple of times, you sort of give up. You don't go around looking and asking the way you did" (NI-46).

A more common Negro reaction to the racial situation is to assume there will be discrimination,[25] that he will be unwelcome, and hence not even to bother trying. "I think a good bit of the discrimination here and elsewhere is the Negro's fault, that he segregates himself and refuses to try things which he hears are closed to him" (NI-33). Or as another Negro said, "I'm quite timid, and just don't see the sense in taking any chances on being hurt or embarrassed" (NI-55). This reaction is found in all areas of behavior, and in many instances is closely tied in with an attitude of resignation. It is especially striking in the case of Southern-born Negroes who are generally more suspicious of whites.[26]

In housing, for example, the following remarks are typical of Negro residents:

"Many Negroes when they come in don't even bother to try buying or renting except from Negroes 'cause everyone tells them they can't and that it's a waste of time trying" (NI-12).

"We'd like another house, but we haven't tried. It's just no use. They won't sell to Negroes" (NI-3).

The same attitude holds for the occupational area of behavior. One finds few Negroes applying for jobs which have not traditionally been theirs. Said one woman, "I'd have liked to work in one of the stores here, but never tried. You have that awful feeling you'll be refused and maybe insulted" (NI-52). Both whites and Negroes realize that the latter have not tried as hard as they might have to find new and better jobs:

"The Wire Mill doesn't hire Negroes, but I know of none who have applied. With regard to that, and to the Market

Basket incident you told me about,* the failure of people to apply or try for jobs has a lot to do with the job pattern. Nobody bothers to try places they think might not hire them" (NI-29).

"There are lots of jobs in town that would take Negroes if they'd just apply for them, but they just assume they can't get them and do nothing about them" (WI-14).

Evidences of this avoidance pattern are also found in both CIO unions. Many Negro men believe, despite signs to the contrary, that certain union positions are not open to them, and many Negro women deliberately exclude themselves from union social activities even when their husbands participate or when invited to do so by whites:

"Union picnics are fine, but the wife has never gone on one. I told her they were O.K., but she didn't want to take a chance" (NI-14).

"I was asked to be on the union bowling team, but had to refuse. I have to cook supper for my husband and the other boarders. Also, something might happen to make me regret it. It's better not to get too close to whites" (NI-26).

If Negroes tend to avoid social contact with whites on such a favorable level, they do so even more in social and religious activities. There is evidence of this fear not only in close personal relations but in the more institutionalized relationships such as the various clubs and organizations, the Red Cross and Visiting Nurse Association, and, of course, the churches. One Catholic said:

"I'm a Catholic, but I've never been to church since I came here. I was told when I first came that Negroes weren't welcome in any of the white churches, and rather than be embarrassed or take a chance on it, I just never went. How would I feel if the priest asked me to leave in front of everybody?" (NI-51).

*See p. 50.

Politics is also generally felt to be forbidden territory aside from voting. Scarcely any Negroes feel any position is available to them, and no Negroes have ever tried for any of these positions.

Finally, this defeatist type of reaction is common with reference to many public facilities. Here are some typical reactions:

"Neither of us have ever tried the barber and beauty shops here because we felt sure they wouldn't serve us. Anyway, it would be a most embarrassing situation" (NI-62, 63).

"I've never been to Pilgrim Head Beach 'cause I heard they did everything possible to discourage Negroes from using it, and I see no sense in looking for trouble" (NI-61).

Consciousness of Kind. This pregnant expression falls in with and is a part of general sociological thinking. It is closely related to ethnocentrism, or Sumner's in-group and out-group dichotomy.[27] It suggests that people prefer their own type, whether of race, class, or nationality. This appears to be a general human trait. To the extent that Negroes have this feeling, it operates largely on a diffuse and unconscious level, reinforcing the segregation pattern. It has a number of various manifestations and is found operating in all areas of behavior.

1. *Other Negroes Not Present.* Many Negroes, particularly those with a Southern background, have a self-consciousness and a desire for protective coloration which manifests itself in a refusal to do things or to go places where other Negroes cannot customarily be found.[28] As one man said, "Although I think whites are mostly to blame for segregation and discrimination, I also think Negroes often tend to segregate themselves from whites. Lots of them, including myself, won't go some place if they see only whites there" (NI-51). Conversely, this sentiment helps explain the tend-

ency of Negroes to flock to any place or organization that accepts them.

This Negro feeling is found in all areas of behavior. It is seen in housing, for example, where Negroes are reluctant to live any great distance from other Negroes. As one Negro said frankly, "If I ever build here, it will be on my own property, right behind the folks' house [in the "segregated" area]. I wouldn't want to live in a white area any more than they would like to live here among us" (NI-42). Other evidences of this attitude are seen where Negroes have had the opportunity and money to buy outside the Negro area, but have refused to do so because they did not wish to live among strangers, and whites at that. Still another example is the statement by one of the white officials of the USW: "If the housing project had gone through, Mr. Beach was in favor of having two separate sections for white and colored. He said it would mean less trouble, and that the colored would feel better with it that way" (WI-84).

In the occupational area of behavior this attitude is found with respect to Negroes working at the Wire Mill, and with respect to Negro women working at the Iron Foundry. As one of the Wire Mill officials said, "We have very few colored applications because people tend to go into work where others of their kind are. In town most colored work at the Iron Foundry, so they go there" (WI-93). As for Negro women working at the Foundry, one young Negro man who works there put it rightly when he said, "Some of the women say they'd feel too lonely being the only colored or nearly so, and so they don't even try. They just bitch" (NI-33). While true, these two statements, as we have seen, are inadequate explanations for the complete absence of these two categories of Negro workers at these two factories.

Even in the educational area this attitude is quite widespread among Negro youth. Although most Negro children do not attend school social events, some go often to dances and dance only with Negroes when it would be perfectly possible and permissible for them to do so with whites. A common Negro attitude is resentfully described by one who is a good bit more emancipated than most:

"School is perfect with absolutely no discrimination from anybody in any of its aspects. My main gripe with the school is that the Negro kids keep so much to themselves. They all come together, go to their classes, and then go home together. They never seem to try and just be one of the gang" (NI-37).

And one mother said:

"The proms are held at the Apple Valley Club, and all students are invited to go, but none of the colored girls ever will. They say they would be the only ones there, and that they'd feel out of place. It makes me so mad. They only bring discrimination and segregation on themselves" (NI-49).

The same attitude prevails for Negro parents not attending or joining the PTA. Said one, "No, I never joined the PTA. None of the others went, and so I didn't either. If I see no other Negroes, I just stay away" (NI-17).

Of course, this point of view is common with respect to social groupings. Thus, in the early days of the Hi-Y, only a few Negroes like Nat Johnson participated. "The others were not so chummy, and kept pretty much to themselves" (WI-79). Today, as mentioned earlier, it has turned into the completely segregated Washington Club "because the Negroes here want to be by themselves" (WI-94).

Finally, politics and public facilities have evidences of this attitude. In the former it has successfully counteracted white invitations to join certain of the Fire Departments. In the latter, mention of it was made with regard to beaches, restaurants, taverns, and the movies. Remarks similar to these were occasionally encountered:

"We went over to Twin Beach once, but didn't see any Negroes there, and so we knew there was no sense in even trying" (NI-17).

"The colored at the movies all sit in groups by themselves. They probably don't have to, but they do it anyway" (NI-58).

"I wish there was a Negro restaurant so we could all go there" (NI-13).

This "wanting to be by themselves," closely related to many other types of Negro support of the race relations pattern, no doubt reflects the feeling of greater ease when Negro is with Negro. The attitude, applicable almost anywhere, is summed up in "I would just rather be among my own people" (NI-57), and well demonstrated by this remark: "We aren't interested in white people or in getting to know them. If a white fellow in the shop asked me home for supper one evening to meet his wife, I'd faint dead away, and when I came to I wouldn't know what to say" (NI-16).

2. *Race Pride.* This feeling[29] was seldom expressed by Negroes. Where found it applied only to some public facilities and in social and religious activities, often in the form of rationalizations. In general, it consists of a feeling of superiority for Negro customs and of contempt for white ones.

Race pride is also closely related to an awareness of race and cultural difference. This can be seen in the preference for Negro barber and beauty shops. Negroes rationalize, possibly correctly, that their hair is different from whites', and whites do not therefore know how to handle it. Said one veteran, "I prefer Negro barbers because I found out in the army that whites didn't know how to give me a good haircut" (NI-43). And one young woman who had once regularly attended a local white church, expressed her preference for St. Andrews in this fashion:

"No, I wouldn't want to go to any of the other churches.

They are O.K., but the services are sort of dry. They read everything, even the prayers, and nobody ever offers their own prayers. They have too many airs, they put on airs, and everyone is scared to breathe or laugh" (NI-50) .

3. *Fear of Public Opinion*. In a sense this reason[30] falls under the general heading of Consciousness of Kind, and is found only in social activities. It is usually seen in the hesitancy of Negro boys to date white girls because, "People talk about you" (NI-67) , and in the unwillingness of Negro adults to be very friendly with whites. As one woman said, "Nobody else does it with their white friends [i.e., invites them to the home for social occasions], so I'd be a little out of place" (NI-39) . Still another example of the pressure of public opinion, operating in reverse, so to speak, is seen in this boy's statement:

"Of my best friends, only one is Negro. I play on Cove and Birch Streets, especially with two boys. We three play together all the time, visit, have snacks, etc. I seldom go over to Western Avenue as they poke fun at me about all my white friends and call me 'Mr. White Man.' Most of them have white friends, too, but not as close ones as me" (NI-72) .

Desire for Paternalism. This form of acceptance of the race relations pattern,[31] which is a desire to avoid challenging it, is found in three areas of behavior: housing, jobs, and religious activities. As usually stated, it expresses a desire to have whites assume more responsibility for Negroes, as for example, "They should have cared for Mrs. Moon when her husband died. The Iron Foundry brought most of the colored up here, and they ought to look after them" (NI-14) . This point of view was more common among Southern-born Negroes who were more accustomed in the light of their own upbringing to having whites assume such responsibilities.

Fear of White Financial Pressure. This feared white pressure exists largely in terms of housing and union activities. Negroes often hesitate to buy into white areas, because, "If you work here, they could put all sorts of pressures on you, and you might even lose your job" (NI-48). They are also afraid to participate in union activities for the same reason. An older Negro resident put it well when he said:

"I could have been a steward but refused to accept it. I broke my leg at the Iron Foundry about ten years ago, and so they gave me a lifetime job. If I was working for the union on any kind of committees, there might be hard feelings, and I have been treated O.K. I wouldn't want to jeopardize my job and financial security" (NI-57).

Personal Pride. The best example of this[32] is seen in housing where Negroes are often too proud to use whites or their favors to overcome white prejudices and discrimination. "No, I'd be too proud to take it" (NI-23), is a typical answer by a man faced with the question of whether he would consider having a white buy for him. This reaction can also be seen occasionally when Negroes refuse to invite whites to their homes. Said one lady, "I've never asked them to visit here. I don't have much to offer them, sitting in the kitchen" (NI-34). The ultimate in this Negro attitude is seen in this statement: "The Connecticut F.E.P.A. law has been a great help to colored in Connecticut because now they can't be refused service. However, what's the use of the law forcing people to serve you? I wouldn't feel right drinking and knowing he was being forced to serve me" (NI-43). Avoidance here is, of course, related to the fear they would not be welcome, just as many other types of avoidance are also interrelated.

Habit and Tradition. This factor[33] is intimately related to avoidance by Negroes of challenges to the race relations pattern. It is found in most human behavior, and seems to be the counterpart of the pressure of the mores which was discussed earlier. It is characteristic of people to form habits and traditions, whatever their status or that of their group, and to follow these accustomed paths. This social inertia is particularly discernible in two areas of behavior. The first of these is the religious. Negroes in many cases have attended the Negro church and stayed away from the white churches because, as one woman said, "I'm a Methodist, and that's my church. It just never occurred to me to go to the church of another denomination" (NI-59). In other words, once a Negro church was founded it was likely that Negroes would continue going there out of habit. As one young Negro said, "Now there's a tradition about our own church, and we'll probably never go back to the other ones" (NI-56).

The other area of behavior, public facilities, involves the use mainly of the barber and beauty shops. Where the Negro concerned is brought up in town, he follows his family's pattern of behavior as did the young woman who remarked, "I never even thought of attending a white beauty parlor here. I just went to the family's old standby in Central City" (NI-13). Where Negroes come to Connecticut Town after they have matured, they are either taken by friends to Negro barbers in Central City, or, being told they cannot be served in town, they go themselves to Central City. "I was taken by relatives to Central City and kept going there" (NI-7). Once this habit is formed, it becomes "the natural thing to do to use Negro barbers" (NI-31).

Vested Interest. Almost an impersonal factor, vested interest[34] is closely related to habit and tradition. It operates to keep a distinction between the races and to maintain Negro avoidance of whites. Since Negroes live largely in a separate social world, parallel institutions have developed which many Negroes find advantageous to maintain. This factor is particularly important in maintaining the race relations pattern in the South, but not in Connecticut Town. The Negro community there is too small and undeveloped to support more than one Negro institution, i.e., the church. Vested interest has, therefore, little chance to operate. The only instance of it involved housing and St. Andrews Church. One of the church officers was asked to find a Negro family which would be willing to move into a white neighborhood in Beach Haven; the white owner there was trying to sell to Negroes to spite his neighbors. One Negro family was already interested, but needed another to complete the arrangement. "Mr. Beach said he knew of someone who might want the other house and insisted on handling it himself. However, he never contacted us or let us know of anyone who might have been interested" (NI-60). In this instance, as reported by Mr. Beach himself, he was reluctant to have local Negroes live so far from the church, fearing that if they did so it would be further weakened. He therefore deliberately sabotaged the effort.

We have seen a general Negro avoidance of challenge to the race relations pattern. What this means is that, by and large, the Negro accepts the pattern established by the dominant group,[35] and goes along with the few favors the whites deign to give him.

A lack of aggressiveness is present throughout the Negro community.[36] It is held mainly by the Southern Negro majority who dominate their community and who tend "to accept things as they are and not to protest or fight against them" (NI-19). This point of view is well expressed in these Negro remarks:

"We're pretty well satisfied as we are, and where we are. We've made the best of what we have, and are pretty well resigned to where we are in life and society. We just try to make the best of it" (NI-20, 21).

"When in Rome, do as the Romans do. I don't want to do anything that might embarrass me" (NI-51).

As we have seen, in housing we find a Negro unwillingness to fight for good homes, an unwillingness to put up with
trouble and hostile neighbors and constant rebuffs in order
to get decent housing. Likewise in the job arena this attitude
is seen where Negroes want certain jobs but are afraid to
ask or fight for them, or where they avoid union contacts
for the same reason. Even the youngsters' school life, as
well as PTA activities, have some of this accommodative
attitude.

Furthermore, acceptance and lack of aggressiveness are
present to a large degree in social and religious activities,
politics, and in the use of public facilities where Negroes
often accept discriminatory treatment without protest.

What are the outward manifestations of this attitude
aside from the avoidance pattern previously mentioned?
They are twofold. The first is a general lack of interest.
This is found in each area of behavior, but particularly in
social and religious activities where it is usually expressed
by "I'm just not interested." Another indication of it is the
use of rationalizations by Negroes to justify their lack of
participation in community activities.

Secondly, it is seen in the almost complete lack of any
local Negro organization, such as the National Association
for the Advancement of Colored People, to work for their
rights and privileges, much less in the presence of any
adequate type of Negro leadership.[37] No organizations exist
outside St. Andrews Church, and St. Andrews is not interested in such worldly matters as civil rights.[38] The leadership available is often rejected by Northern Negroes who
feel it is lacking in too many respects such as education and
a real interest in civil rights. As one white politician com-
mented, "They're without real leadership and are very un-
organized, and never look for anything that I know of"
(WI-65) . What this adds up to is that the local Negroes are

not sufficiently dissatisfied with their present status to try to do something about it, or else feel that it is a hopeless task.[39]

Thus, social control consists of more than pressure by one group on another group. Instead, it operates through four separate though interrelated processes: the impersonal factors, the influence of the mores on whites (including general white ignorance and indifference), the dynamic actions by whites against Negroes, and the self-imposed segregation of the Negroes. What was especially revealing were the impersonal factors and the self-segregating role of the Negro. The white pressures and attitudes on both white and Negro were much as expected.

With respect to the impersonal factors, Negroes are less educated and trained, less wealthy, and less responsible and dependable than whites. These handicaps are compounded because most Negroes are new to town, and so are regarded with suspicion by most whites. Finally, while Negro numbers are so small that Negroes have little political or other influence, they have increased so fast that the town is particularly aware of their presence. All these factors tend to structure the situation against the Negro before he is subjected to any form of pressure.

The white mores tend to keep whites and Negroes apart even while the individual white seems somewhat uncertain about both what the mores and the race relations pattern are. The situation is further confused by the fact that while the mores are closely related to white rationalizations for maintaining discrimination, it is often difficult to distinguish between them.

The white control techniques are the most common method of keeping separate "places" for whites and Negroes. These techniques are customarily the final pressures applied, and are generally used only when the other types of control have failed. These white controls run the gamut from the most overt to the most subtle type of action. They consist mostly of subtle, informal, and noninstitutionalized pressures although there are formal and institutionalized pressures as well. The more extreme measures are taken only when the gentler ones have failed. Even then, such techniques as violence are usually not necessary to maintain the race relations pattern. The fact that such practices have occasionally been used in other places, as for example in Cicero, Illinois, several years ago, seems to have the effect of deterring subordinate groups in places like Connecticut Town from potentially hazardous actions. White behavior is also marked by ignorance and lack of concern about Negroes. This also serves as a control function since it helps to perpetuate the race situation.

Finally, it seems that self-control by a minority group may be an important factor in maintaining the status quo. This self-control develops out of experience and is perpetuated by continuing socialization. The Negro adjusts more to the race pattern than does the white, and his acceptance of the pattern helps to perpetuate it. This Negro self-control is based in part on what he thinks the situation to be. In this he may be mistaken, reacting toward an imaginary rather than a real situation. The Negro just assumes, for example, that he cannot work at certain jobs or in certain places. He therefore does not apply, although there may actually be no barrier against him.

This Negro self-control usually takes the form of avoidance of whites by Negroes. This can be done through migration, complete or segmental, or simply by withdrawing from participation in community activities. It takes place for a variety of reasons, the most common of which are fear of rebuff and awareness of race. Finally, this self-control results in a lack of aggressiveness, a lack of interest in the community and its activities, and a lack of Negro organization and leadership capable of challenging the status quo.

CHAPTER FIVE

Summary and Interpretations

In our introductory chapter the problems to be investigated were posed in this way. First, what is the Negro's "place" in Connecticut Town? What is the race relations pattern, and does it differ in the various areas of behavior? This meant determining the degree of subordination and exclusion of Negroes as well as the extent to which they participate in community activities relative to whites.

Secondly, what are the means used to maintain the existing race relations pattern; what processes of social control operate to keep Negroes "in their place"? This does not mean that we ignored the forces operating on whites to keep them "in *their* place," for in a sense this is the effect of the mores on whites. Rather, it means that by looking for evidences of pressures against Negroes aiming to perpetuate segregation, we were better able to pinpoint our efforts.

What general conclusions can be drawn about the race relations situation? It has already been noted that the relative status of the two races cannot be precisely described. This is so for two reasons: (1) it varies from one area of behavior to another; and (2) with the possible exception of education, the Negro's "place" cannot be precisely defined, even in any single area of behavior.

There are no laws in Connecticut Town establishing any specific status for the Negro except as a complete equal. At the same time, the fairly recent passage in the North of state or city laws banning discrimination in employ-

ment, educational institutions, and public facilities is indirect evidence of discrimination. In short, the status of
the Negro in the North, as seen in towns of this type, is
similar in many ways to that in the South as revealed in
many other studies.[1] The basic difference between the two
areas seems to be that Connecticut Town's "place" definition of the Negro is less clear in detail and there is less
consensus regarding it in either the white or Negro community. As a result, there is much more possibility for
deviation. We have seen how it is possible for the individual Negro to stretch the limits of his "place" definition,
and at certain places and times to break through the barriers imposed on him. He thus deviates from the pattern,
often because of outstanding personality or ability, or a
personal acquaintanceship with the white involved in the
situation. Such a person tends to serve as a positive contrast to the mass of Negroes and is considered "different."
Thus, paradoxically, he demonstrates the continued vigor
of the traditional status definition, even while he suggests
that this definition lacks the full force of the mores, and
may, as conditions alter, be susceptible to change.

As for the processes of social control, the low socioeconomic
status of the Negro has already been cited as one factor. Behind this may be found a denial of equal opportunities in
the past. But the fact remains that this factor tends partially
to prohibit the Negro from participating in society to the
same extent as whites. He cannot get the housing he needs
and suffers more from the housing shortage; he is forced
into certain types of jobs not always wholly desirable; certain
social, religious, and political activities are completely closed
to him; and certain public facilities are more inaccessible to
him—all these things, in part at least, because of his social
and cultural background rather than because of white racist
attitudes.

Further, his largely nonlocal background—what Cox refers to as the Stranger Situation[2]—which is mainly of Southern origin, results in greater suspicion and aloofness toward him than might otherwise be the case. His position in Connecticut Town is analogous to, if not identical with, that of other immigrants. He faces the barrier of ethnocentrism, perhaps in a peculiarly difficult form. Because he is in fact foreign, he arouses the antagonisms which universally greet the foreigner even though he is not recognized as a cultural alien. Therefore his unfamiliar and inept behavior is attributed to his race, and he is not regarded as eligible for the melting pot which is supposed to transform other outlanders into acceptable members of the in-group. Moreover, the fact that he does not possess the cultural "know-how," when added to the knowledge that he always risks painful rebuffs, makes him hesitate to participate in community affairs, in social activities, and even to try for job opportunities which might actually be available to him.

This situation is worsened by the doubling and tripling of his numbers from 1910 to 1920 and 1930 respectively. This rapid increase, while still leaving him a relatively insignificant part of the total population, is apparently greatly responsible for the increased suspicion and discrimination which he encounters today. It might be said that this increase is the final "straw that broke the camel's back."

Where white pressures on whites are concerned, i.e., the control of the mores over whites, the individual white appears to be uncertain in his own mind about both the mores and the actual pattern of race relations. What he thinks is the situation, or what he says is the situation, is often in conflict with his own personal feelings, or the conflict may be the result of his overestimating the intolerance of other whites.[3] Many whites remark that while they would not mind having Negroes of their own socioeconomic class move into their neighborhood, they "know" that their neighbors would object. In other words, the members of a given group act not only in terms of those mores which actually exist, but also in terms of those thought to exist. Representing a more or less extreme form of public opinion, real or imaginary, the mores tend to keep members of the white community set apart from Negroes and to make it virtually impossible for them to participate equally with Negroes in most areas of behavior.

The mores, of course, are closely related to the white rationalizations, and in some instances it is hard to distinguish between them. Thus, when presented with the question of hiring or serving Negroes, it is interesting to note that the whites often are not defensive. They say they cannot do one or the other because their customers will not like it. To them this is a patent, self-evident truth; to the observer it is not always so clear.

It is likewise interesting to note that the value systems and rationalizations of whites differ from one area of behavior to another. In one case they provide for discrimination; in another, they do not. Compare, for example, the values of the educational system as opposed to the occupational area of behavior, or those of the church as opposed to the public facilities. In other words, the traditions reflected in rationalizations are specific as to time, place, and situation.

The result of these different value systems is that the white techniques for control of the Negroes often vary from one area of behavior to another. The more important the area and its emotional content, the more likely it is that whites will take extreme action. Thus, with all that one's home implies in America in terms of family and property values, it is not surprising that it is only here where violence has been suggested or where economic pressure has been brought to bear. The same is true of those particularly sensitive public facilities such as barber shops and bars where insults are frequently resorted to in the attempt to keep Negroes out. However, as has been suggested previously, these techniques are greatly tempered by Negro attitudes and behavior toward the race relations pattern. It might be expected, for example, that some of the more extreme white techniques would be manifested in the area of social and religious activities. That this has not been the case is not due so much to white restraint as to the fact that Negroes have not tried to participate in these activities. In any case, the controls exercised by whites are generally loose, informal, and ill-defined.

This brings us to the general Negro acceptance of the race pattern. On an interpretative level it may be inferred that for the Negro to stay "in his place," gives him a sense of security in that he knows what is normally expected of him and what he may legitimately expect from others. In short, he knows how to act toward those in a dominant position. In the North, on the other hand, numerous instances constantly occur where the Negro does not know what to expect. This may be just what some Negroes mean when they say, "Down South as long as Negroes stay 'in their place' they're served O.K. Here you never know what will happen or how you'll be treated" (NI-14). They thus suggest that in some ways the South is a better place in which to live: their "place" is more clearly defined.

Parallel with the pressures which the dominant group exerts on its members are the pressures the Negro group exerts on *its* members. These pressures, which strengthen group identification, are effective because in-group membership is a source of security and rewards. Consciousness of kind then becomes theoretically relevant. We can see from other studies as well as our own that social barriers, differences in kind, are not based solely on racial stigmata. As

Wirth has pointed out, the in-group may be a place where the individual can relax into warm, friendly, spontaneous relations and, in a sense, let down his guard.[4] In any case, whether or not the Negro explicitly accepts the majority group definition of his status, he may develop a conception of himself and a persistent awareness of himself as a Negro. This awareness is a social product arising from his interaction with both Negroes and whites.

Thus, in the process of adjustment to the biracial situation, the Negro learns to set limits to his goals. He may learn this either directly from experiences at the hands of whites, or indirectly from Negroes recounting their own experiences and giving advice. He develops a set of anticipatory responses which inhibit his behavior where whites are involved. He will not apply to this company, or for this job, or seek service in this public facility, for fear of suffering embarrassment or humiliation. This being the case, almost any effort on the part of a Negro to achieve positions not customarily held by Negroes in the community involves a definite, conscious, and persistent rejection of the existing barriers. Not many are willing to do this. As the common saying goes, they want advancement but not martyrdom. Consequently, even in the North and in towns like this one, the Negro learns to avoid types of behavior and situations which he believes are potentially painful. Instead, he takes the line of least resistance. The punishment which he may receive for stepping out of his "place" may consist not only of actual rejection by whites but also fear of the same. The fact that there is no clearly defined pattern of discrimination in the bars, for example, makes for insecurity and avoidance on the part of many local Negroes; while out-of-towners, not knowing any better, patronize them. As some Negro informants said, when they go for a beer all they want is to drink and have a good time. They are not interested in a reform crusade; they do not want trouble and embarrass-ment. They want to enjoy themselves, not pioneer in race relations. Thus, this self-imposed restraint is a sort of built-in form of social control.

Before taking a look at what the future may hold for race relations in Connecticut Town, it is worth while to consider one additional aspect of the situation. The question to be asked is, to what extent values are shared by both Negroes and whites. To the degree that this happens it is an aspect of acceptance by Negroes of the race relations pattern. The implication here is that social control is built on consensus and agreement between Negroes and whites on certain under-lying ideas which serve as premises for the rationalizations employed by both groups. In this situation the subordinate group shares the premises of the dominant group and vice versa. The rationalizations of both groups thus provide the basis for rapport because they are efforts to justify the be-havior of each group.

This reciprocal symmetry of underlying premises can be seen in a number of different aspects of the race relations pattern. For example, both races exhibit a good deal of indifference about the relative status and position of the Negro. Both races have, for certain individuals at least, the same favorable attitudes toward paternalism; and they both seem to anticipate that violence is one of the techniques which might be appropriate to maintain control. At the other extreme, both Negroes and whites agree that participa-tion in social and religious occasions is more comfortable when one is with "his own people." These instances could be duplicated in other ways, but are sufficient to demonstrate that the racial pattern persists because both groups agree in large measure on the same set of values for the different areas of behavior. In this fashion, members of both groups are not continually called upon for strong action to preserve the status quo, and life can go on in a more routine and traditional fashion without the constant necessity of solving new problems.

In all of this there is the possibility of change. This can occur in one of two ways. The first of these is what might be called the general climate of the times, and is based on these four factors: (1) a nondiscriminatory school policy; (2) the emergence of outstanding and personable Negroes; (3) the almost continuous high level of employment which began during World War II and which has resulted in increased job opportunities, better pay, and enhanced seniority for Negroes; and (4) the rising Negro educational level.

With regard to the first of these, it is hard to see how successive generations so educated can help but adopt increasingly liberal attitudes. Certainly this has been the case in this country over at least the last twenty years, even though, as we have noted, value systems differ from one area of behavior to another and are not necessarily carried over from one to another. Secondly, in the course of this study a number of examples have been given of the extent to which whites are willing to accept Negroes of unusual talent and personality in areas of behavior hitherto barred to their race. This fact will undoubtedly continue and possibly even develop a cumulative effect.

The third factor has had few local manifestations. Among the few such evidences were the hiring of Negroes by the Toy Factory for the first time, the creation of a state F.E.P.A. law, and the increasing willingness of the Iron Foundry to hire Negro women and to promote Negro men. But these pieces of evidence cannot be positively affirmed. As we have seen, the over-all race pattern has not altered radically since the early 1940's. However, the increasing shortage of adequately trained and skilled men throughout the United

States is bound, even if only in a limited fashion, to make its effect felt in Connecticut Town.

Fourth, as to the rising Negro educational level, it can easily be seen what the future promises here. While no local Negro over 50 years of age ever went beyond ninth grade, over 50 percent of those under 21 have gone, or are realistically planning to go, beyond the twelfth grade. As their educational background improves, local Negroes will undoubtedly be more easily accepted and will more easily acquire the cultural patterns of the community.[5] Yet, in view of the local job situation, those best educated may have to leave in order to find suitable jobs, while the less well-educated remain. This characteristic is a distinctive feature of small towns anywhere, for white as well as for Negro.[6] The result is that while improved educational standing will help the over-all status of the Negro in America and in the large cities, his small town status may lag considerably behind that of the rest of the country. This is so, not only because of limited job opportunities for Negro youth, but also because in a sense the small community of this sort is isolated from the national culture. It is in a backwash, and develops and perpetuates its own race relations pattern.

Apart from these factors relating to the general climate of the times, change may also occur through Negro resistance to discrimination. As one young Negro, most of whose social and religious activities take place in Central City, has remarked, "Try anything and fight for your rights. Act as if you wanted something, and you're likely to get it" (NI-18).[7] Isolated instances of this type of Negro reaction were found in five areas of behavior and have taken several different forms. They can probably be counted upon to increase in the future. For example, Negroes may learn to take more advantage of the F.E.P.A. law.

Negro resistance can also take advantage of white support.

One example, in housing, is what is called "buying for an undisclosed principal," that is, having a white buy for the Negro. This is customarily done by a lawyer or by some acquaintance of the Negro, but is almost invariably practiced by nonlocal Negroes. Still another instance is seen in this case involving use of the public facilities:

"The Spring Restaurant used to smash glasses used by Negroes and to refuse service. Their excuse was that we were drunk. It worked all right until they pulled it on me one time, and I protested to [a town official]. He threatened to revoke their license if it continued. I understand everything is all right now" (NI-8).

On the other hand, Negro resistance need not always depend on white support. In the most common case, the Negro threatens violence if the discriminatory practice continues: "There used to be some name-calling, but I told them I'd knock their heads off if they did it again, and they never did" (NI-11). In another instance, if the Negro is able, he "passes" for white, either temporarily or permanently; this has allegedly occurred only twice in Connecticut Town Finally, the Negro can insist on participating in a certain activity whether whites like it or not, as occurred in the case of the one Negro who is a member of the Town Band.

In conclusion, in examining the processes of social control, we have seen that some are unconscious while others are conscious, some are vague and diffused while others are specific and deliberate, some are subtle while others are overt and crude, some are indirect while others are direct. In general, it seems that in such a town as this one, social control in race relations tends to be unofficial, informal, situational, subtle, and indirect.

Further, we have seen how the race relations pattern is not one merely imposed by whites on Negroes, but is also due in important respects to the operation of socioeconomic differences between the races and to the segregating actions of Negroes themselves. With reference to the controls exercised by whites, no particular types of controls were restricted to this or that socioeconomic class of whites. On the other hand, this would probably not be the case for either Negro acquiescence or resistance. Here it would seem that the greater the education and training and the higher the socioeconomic position of the Negro, the more positive and deliberate would be his resistance as contrasted with the withdrawal pattern. Both these last-named points need further study and examination before they can be more definitely affirmed.

Thus, social control is seen to be a most complex mechanism and the theory of social control to be capable of refinement and further interpretation, as this study has suggested. Theoretically and practically speaking, many of our findings would appear to be worthy of further study. For example, the "Rank Order of Discriminations" found in our areas of behavior needs further corroboration, as do the relative parts played in social control by the four factors mentioned above. This is particularly true where the main theoretical contributions of this study are concerned, i.e., the importance of the impersonal factors and the self-imposed segregation of the Negro in the perpetuation of the race relations pattern.

Appendices

Appendix A

Informant Number

1   Elderly widow from North. Local resident for over 30 years. Lives outside "segregated" area. Home owner. Less than 8th grade education. Does domestic work. Active in A. M. E. Zion Church. Quoted on pp. 45 and 80.

2   Elderly widow from South. Local resident for over 10 years. Lives outside "segregated" area. Less than 8th grade education. Does domestic work. Active in A. M. E. Zion Church.

3,4   Elderly couple from foreign country. Local residents for less than 5 years. Live inside "segregated" area. Less than 8th grade education. Husband unskilled worker at Iron Foundry. Participate in no local social or religious activities. Members of out-of-town church. Quoted on p. 112.

5   Elderly bachelor from South. Local resident for over 25 years. Lives inside "segregated" area. 9th grade education. Semiskilled worker at Iron Foundry. Active in A. M. E. Zion Church. Quoted on pp. 53 and 80.

6   Elderly widow from North. Local resident for over 50 years. Lives outside "segregated" area. 9th grade education. Active in A. M. E. Zion Church.

7   Young bachelor from South. Local resident for less than 5 years. Lives outside "segregated" area. 10th grade education. Semiskilled worker at Iron Foundry. Active in A. M. E. Zion Church. Quoted on p. 120.

8,9   Middle-aged couple from South. Local residents for over 5 years. Live inside "segregated" area. Home owners. 10th and 9th grade education respectively. Husband professional man. Active in A. M. E. Zion Church. Quoted on pp. 91 and 134.

10   Young bachelor from North. Local resident for less than 5 years. Lives inside "segregated" area. 14th grade educa-

tion. Semiskilled worker at Iron Foundry. Participates in no local religious activities. Quoted on p. 40.

11   Middle-aged divorcée from South. Local resident for over 35 years. Lives inside "segregated" area. Home owner. Less than 8th grade education. Semiskilled worker at Shirt Factory. Active in A. M. E. Zion Church. Quoted on pp. 100-101 and 134.

12   Middle-aged bachelor from South. Local resident for less than 5 years. Lives inside "segregated" area. Less than 8th grade education. Semiskilled worker at Iron Foundry. Active in A. M. E. Zion Church. Quoted on pp. 45, 108, and 112.

13   Young locally-born woman. Lives outside "segregated" area. 14th grade education. Still studying. Active in A. M. E. Zion Church. Member of Junior Musical Society (white organization). Quoted on pp. 117 and 120.

14,15   Middle-aged couple from South. Local residents for over 5 years. Live inside "segregated" area. 14th and 12th grade education respectively. Husband semiskilled worker at Iron Foundry. Wife does domestic work. Wife active in A. M. E. Zion Church. Quoted on pp. 41, 47, 95, 109-110, 113, 118, and 129.

16,17   Middle-aged couple from South. Local residents for over 10 years. Live inside "segregated" area. Less than 8th and 8th grade education respectively. Husband semiskilled worker at Iron Foundry. Wife does domestic work. Members of A. M. E. Zion Church. Quoted on pp. 95, 116, and 117.

18,19   Young couple from New England. Local residents for less than 5 years. Live outside "segregated" area. 9th and 10th grade education respectively. Semiskilled workers out-of-town. Participate in no local social or religious activities. Quoted on pp. 70, 99, 121, and 133.

20,21   Elderly couple from South and North respectively. Local residents for over 10 years. Live inside "segregated" area. Less than 8th grade education. Husband unskilled worker at Iron Foundry. Wife does domestic work. Active in A. M. E. Zion Church. Quoted on pp. 41-42, 58, 102, 105-106, 109, and 121.

22   Elderly widow from South. Local resident for over 5

years. Lives inside "segregated" area. Less than 8th grade education. Active in A. M. E. Zion Church.

23,24 Elderly couple from South. Local residents for over 5 years. Live inside "segregated" area. Less than 8th grade education. Husband semiskilled worker at Iron Foundry. Wife unskilled worker at Shirt Factory. Participate in no local religious activities. Quoted on pp. 43 and 119.

25,26 Young couple from South. Local residents for over 5 years. Live inside "segregated" area. Less than 8th and 12th grade education respectively. Husband semiskilled worker at Iron Foundry. Wife semiskilled worker at Shirt Factory. Participate in no local religious activities. Quoted on p. 113.

27 Elderly bachelor from South. Local resident for over 25 years. Lives inside "segregated" area. Less than 8th grade education. Unskilled worker at Iron Foundry. Member of A. M. E. Zion Church.

28 Middle-aged bachelor from South. Local resident for less than 5 years. Lives inside "segregated" area. 12th grade education. Semiskilled worker at Iron Foundry. Participates in no local religious activities.

29,30 Young couple from South and Connecticut Town respectively. Local residents for over 10 years. Live out-of-town. Less than 8th and 13th grade education respectively. Husband semiskilled worker at Iron Foundry. Wife skilled worker out-of-town. Previously active in A.M.E. Zion Church. Have close white friends. Quoted on pp. 93, 100, 107, and 112-113.

31,32 Young couple from South. Local residents for less than 10 years. Live inside "segregated" area. Less than 8th and 8th grade education respectively. Husband semiskilled worker at Iron Foundry. Participate in no local religious activities. Quoted on pp. 108 and 120.

33 Young divorcé from South. Local resident for less than 5 years. Lives inside "segregated" area. 12th grade education. Semiskilled worker at Iron Foundry. Participates in no local religious activities. Quoted on pp. 112 and 115.

34 Middle-aged widow from South. Local resident for over 5 years. Lives inside "segregated" area. 8th grade educa-

tion. Does domestic work. Participates in no local religious activities. Member of out-of-town church. Quoted on pp. 42 and 119.

35 Young widow from North. Local resident for over 5 years. Lives inside "segregated" area. 9th grade education. Does domestic work. Participates in no local religious activities. Member of out-of-town church.

36 Middle-aged widow from South. Local resident for over 10 years. Lives inside "segregated" area. Less than 8th grade education. Semiskilled worker at Shirt Factory. Active in A. M. E. Zion Church. Quoted on pp. 30 and 79.

37 Young bachelor from South. Local resident for over 5 years. Lives inside "segregated" area. 12th grade education. Skilled worker at Printing Company. Participates in no local religious activities. Has close white friends. Quoted on pp. 61, 106, and 116.

38 Middle-aged widow from South. Local resident for over 20 years. Lives inside "segregated" area. Less than 8th grade education. Member of A. M. E. Zion Church. Quoted on p. 82.

39 Middle-aged divorcée from South. Local resident for over 5 years. Lives inside "segregated" area. Less than 8th grade education. Semiskilled worker at Shirt Factory. Member of A. M. E. Zion Church. Quoted on pp. 49 and 118.

40,41 Middle-aged couple from foreign country and New England respectively. Local residents for over 25 years. Live outside "segregated" area. Home owners. Less than 8th and 8th grade education respectively. Husband does private work; is also unskilled worker at Iron Foundry. Husband Roman Catholic. Wife member of A. M. E. Zion Church. Quoted on pp. 29, 43, 66-67, and 84.

42 Young locally-born bachelor. Lives inside "segregated" area. 12th grade education. Previously semiskilled worker at Iron Foundry. Now in Armed Forces. Member of A. M. E. Zion Church. Quoted on pp. 58, 60-61, and 115.

43,44 Young couple from South and North respectively. Local residents for over 5 years. Live inside "segregated" area. 11th and 12th grade education respectively. Husband semiskilled worker at Iron Foundry. Wife semiskilled worker at Shirt Factory. Members of A. M. E. Zion Church. Quoted on pp. 117 and 119.

45   Locally-born youth. Lives inside "segregated" area. 12th grade education. Semiskilled worker at Iron Foundry. Active in A. M. E. Zion Church.

46,47 Middle-aged couple from South and Connecticut respectively. Local residents for over 25 years. Live outside "segregated" area. Home owners. 8th and 10th grade education respectively. Husband factory foreman. Members of A. M. E. Zion Church. Quoted on pp. 59, 106-107, and 112.

48,49 Middle-aged couple from Connecticut Town and South respectively. Local residents for over 15 years. Live outside "segregated" area. 12th and 10th grade education respectively. Husband semiskilled worker for construction company. Wife does domestic work. Members of A. M. E. Zion Church. Quoted on pp. 47, 93, 116, and 119.

50   Young locally-born woman. Lives outside "segregated" area. 10th grade education. Works in store. Active in A. M. E. Zion Church. Quoted on pp. 45, 80, 91, 94, 102, and 117-118.

51,52 Young couple from foreign country. Local residents for over 5 years. Live inside "segregated" area. 8th and less than 8th grade education respectively. Husband semiskilled worker at Iron Foundry. Wife does domestic work. Husband Roman Catholic. Participate in no local religious activities. Quoted on pp. 103, 112, 113, 114, and 121.

53,54 Young couple from South. Local residents for less than 5 years. 8th and 12th grade education respectively. Do domestic work. Members of A. M. E. Zion Church.

55   Middle-aged widow from South. Local resident for less than 5 years. 12th grade education. Does domestic work. Member of A. M. E. Zion Church. Quoted on pp. 106 and 111-112.

56   Locally-born youth. Lives outside "segregated" area. Now in college. Was class officer of Junior and Senior High School classes, co-captain of an athletic team.

Summertime truck driver for construction company. Active in A. M. E. Zion Church. Was officer in Junior Council of Churches. Has many close white friends. Quoted on p. 120.

57,58   Middle-aged couple from South. Local residents for over 25 years. Live outside "segregated" area. Home owners. Less than 8th grade education. Husband semiskilled worker at Iron Foundry. Wife does laundry work. Active in A. M. E. Zion Church. Have good white friends and neighbors. Quoted on pp. 34, 81, 93, 102, 103, 117, and 119.

59   Elderly widow from North. Local summertime resident for over 40 years. Lives outside "segregated" area. Home owner. 8th grade education. Member of A. M. E. Zion Church. Quoted on p. 120.

60,61   Young couple from South. Local residents for over 5 years. Live inside "segregated" area. Home owners. 12th and 11th grade education respectively. Husband semiskilled worker at Iron Foundry. Members of A. M. E. Zion Church. Quoted on pp. 43-44, 55, 81, 95, 103, 104, 114, and 121.

62,63   Young couple from South and North respectively. Local residents for over 5 years. Live outside "segregated" area. 9th and 11th grade education respectively. Husband semiskilled worker at Iron Foundry. Participate in no local religious activities. Members of out-of-town church. Wife has good white friends. Quoted on pp. 46, 58, 68, 81, 92, 93, 94, 101, 106, 108-109, and 114.

64,65   Middle-aged couple from North. Local residents for over 5 years. Live outside "segregated" area. 10th and 8th grade education respectively. Husband does domestic work. Participate in no local religious activities. Members of Rocky Ledge Congregational Church. Husband member of Town Band. Have good white friends. Quoted on pp. 41, 59, and 106.

66   Locally-born youth. Lives inside "segregated" area. Now in grade school. Planning to complete high school. Has few white friends, but best friend is white. Plays all sports. Quoted on p. 29.

67   Youth from South. Local resident for over 5 years. Lives

inside "segregated" area. Now in grade school. Planning to complete high school. Is class officer, and captain of an athletic team. Most friends are white. Quoted on p. 118.

68 Locally-born youth. Lives outside "segregated" area. Now in high school. Planning to complete college. Is class officer and co-captain of an athletic team. Active in A.M.E. Zion Church. Most friends are white. Quoted on p. 54.

69 Youth from South. Local resident for less than 5 years. Lives inside "segregated" area. Now in high school. Planning to complete college. Is class officer, officer of Prom Committee, on football and baseball teams, member of Referees Club. Most friends are white.

70 Locally-born youth. Lives inside "segregated" area. Now in grade school. Planning to complete high school. Is captain of an athletic team. Has some white friends. Is on American Legion [Children's] Baseball Club.

71 Locally-born youth. Lives inside "segregated" area. Now in grade school. Planning to complete high school. Is captain of an athletic team, officer of Picnic Committee of his grade. Has some white friends. Best friend is white. Is on American Legion [Children's] Baseball Club.

72 Locally-born youth. Lives inside "segregated" area. Now in grade school. Planning to complete high school. Is on football, basketball, and baseball teams. Most best friends are white. Is member of white Boy Scout troop. Quoted on p. 118.

73 Locally-born youth. Lives inside "segregated" area. Now in high school. Planning to complete junior college. Is class officer, on basketball and baseball teams, member of Referees Club and Glee Club. Has a few white friends. Is on American Legion [Children's] Baseball Club.

74 Locally-born girl. Lives outside "segregated" area. Now in high school. Planning to complete junior college. Is captain of an athletic team, member of Prom Decorating Committee, officer of Service Squad. Active in A. M. E. Zion Church. Has some white friends.

75 Locally-born youth. Lives inside "segregated" area. Now in high school. Is on football and basketball teams,

member of Prom Decorating Committee. Active in A. M. E. Zion Church. Has one white friend. Quoted on p. 60.

76 Locally-born girl. Lives outside "segregated" area. Now in grade school. Planning to complete college. Is officer of Social Committee, member of Glee Club. Active in A. M. E. Zion Church. Most friends are white. Is member of white Girl Scout troop, officer of Junior Musical Society (white organization). Quoted on p. 61.

77 Locally-born youth. Lives outside "segregated" area. Now in high school. Planning to leave school. Is member of Referees Club, Glee Club. Active in A.M.E. Zion Church. Has some white friends.

78 Young husband from South. Local resident for over 5 years. Lives inside "segregated" area. 8th grade education. Semiskilled worker at Iron Foundry. Member of A. M. E. Zion Church. Quoted on p. 41.

Appendix B

Informant Number

1,2 Elderly couple of Russian and French backgrounds respectively. Local residents for over 30 years. Home owners. Owners of small company. Less than 8th grade and 8th grade education respectively. Jewish. Husband member of Rotary, Chamber of Commerce, and Masons.

3 Middle-aged locally-born man of Swedish background. Home owner. Store manager. 8th grade education. Officer in Lutheran Church. Quoted on p. 90.

4 Middle-aged man of Italian background. Local resident for over 25 years. Home owner. Manager of small company. Graduate training. Member of P.T.A. Roman Catholic. Officer in Young Republican Club.

5 Middle-aged man of Swedish background commuting from out-of-town. Local worker for less than 5 years. Store owner. College graduate. Member of Chamber of Commerce.

6 Middle-aged locally-born woman of German-English background. Home owner. Shop owner. 12th grade education. Organizer of P.T.A. Episcopalian.

7 Middle-aged man of Italian background commuting from out-of-town. Local worker for less than 5 years. Tavern owner. 8th grade education. Roman Catholic.

8 Middle-aged man of Scottish background. Local resident for over 10 years. Store owner. College graduate. Roman Catholic. Officer of Rotary, member of Gun Club. Quoted on p. 107.

9 Middle-aged man of French-English background. Local resident for less than 5 years. Restaurant owner. 13th grade education. Episcopalian. Member of the Grange, Chamber of Commerce, and the Restaurant Guild.

10,11 Elderly couple of Yankee and Irish backgrounds respectively. Local residents for over 30 years. Home owners. Store owners. 14th grade education. Episcopalian and Roman Catholic respectively.

12 Middle-aged locally-born man of Yankee background. Home owner. Store owner. 12th grade education. Member of P.T.A. Congregationalist. Member of Rotary and Masons. Quoted on p. 86.

13 Young man of French-Canadian background. Local resident for over 10 years. Store owner. 9th grade education. Roman Catholic. Member of Chamber of Commerce, Exchange Club, Disabled American Veterans, and Veterans of World War II. Member of Auxiliary Police and Civil Defense organization.

14 Middle-aged locally-born woman of Yankee background. Home owner. Store owner. College graduate. Jewish. Quoted on p. 113.

15 Elderly man of Italian background. Local resident for over 35 years. Home owner. Shop owner. Less than 8th grade education. Roman Catholic. Officer of Italian-American Club.

16 Middle-aged man of Italian background. Local resident for over 40 years. Home owner. Shop owner. Less than 8th grade education. Episcopalian. Member of Masons. Former holder of public office. Quoted on pp. 69 and 95.

17 Elderly locally-born man of Irish background. Home owner. Store manager. 8th grade education. Roman Catholic. Member of Knights of Columbus, St. Mary's Holy Name Society, and Chamber of Commerce.

18 Middle-aged man of Yankee background. Local resident for over 20 years. Store manager. 10th grade education. Congregationalist. Member of Chamber of Commerce.

19 Middle-aged locally-born man of Polish background. Home owner. Tavern owner. 13th grade education. Roman Catholic. Member of Croatian Fraternal Union. Former Post Office clerk. Member of Fire Department. Quoted on p. 94.

20 Middle-aged man of Italian background. Local resident for over 30 years. Home owner. Shop owner. 8th grade education. Roman Catholic. Officer of Italian-American Club, member of Gun Club. Quoted on pp. 89 and 105.

21   Young man of Scotch-English background. Local resident
      for over 15 years. Home owner. Lawyer and realty and
      insurance man. Graduate training. Officer in Congrega-
      tional Church. Member of Rotary, Masons, Pilgrim
      Brotherhood, American Legion, and Veterans of World
      War II. Town Judge and Justice of Peace. Quoted on
      p. 83.

22   Elderly man of Yankee background. Local resident for
      over 15 years. Home owner. Store owner. College grad-
      uate. Officer in Rocky Ledge Congregational Church.
      Officer of Rotary and Grange, member of Masons.

23   Middle-aged man of Russian background. Local resident
      for over 25 years. Professional man. Graduate training.
      Jewish. Officer of Rotary, member of American Legion
      and Gun Club. Quoted on p. 90.

24   Middle-aged man of Czechoslovakian background. Local
      resident for over 10 years. Home owner. Store owner.
      College graduate. Roman Catholic. Member of Exchange
      Club.

25   Young man of Russian background commuting from
      out-of-town. Local worker for less than 5 years. Store
      owner. 14th grade education. Jewish. Member of Cham-
      ber of Commerce. Quoted on pp. 88-89.

26   Middle-aged man of Yankee background. Local resident
      for over 35 years. Home owner. Store owner and officer
      of bank. 12th grade education. Baptist. Former officer of
      Masons, American Legion, and Chamber of Commerce.
      Member of Pilgrim Brotherhood. Former holder of public
      office. Quoted on pp. 66 and 70.

27   Young man of Italian background commuting from out-
      of-town. Local worker for less than 5 years. Store owner.
      College graduate. Roman Catholic. Member of Chamber
      of Commerce.

28   Middle-aged locally-born man of Lithuanian background.
      Store manager. 8th grade education. Roman Catholic.

29   Middle-aged man of Czechoslovakian background. Local
      resident for over 15 years. Home owner. Store owner.
      11th grade education. Jewish. Officer of Exchange Club,
      member of Rotary and Chamber of Commerce.

30   Middle-aged locally-born man of English-Irish back-

ground. Home owner. Tavern owner. 12th grade education. Roman Catholic. Former holder of public office. Quoted on p. 90.

31 Young man of Yankee background. Local resident for over 10 years. Home owner. Store owner. 12th grade education. Episcopalian.

32 Middle-aged man of Yankee background. Local resident for less than 5 years. Home owner. Officer of public utility. College graduate. Congregationalist. Officer of Rotary, member of Chamber of Commerce and Pilgrim Brotherhood.

33 Middle-aged locally-born man of French-Canadian background. Home owner. Lawyer and officer of bank. Graduate training. Roman Catholic. Former officer of Knights of Columbus and Rotary, member of Chamber of Commerce. Town judge and former holder of public office.

34 Young man of English-Lebanese background. Local resident for over 5 years. Professional man. College graduate. Roman Catholic. Member of Knights of Columbus and St. Mary's Holy Name Society.

35 Middle-aged locally-born man of Yankee-German background. Home owner. Officer of bank and of real estate and investment company. College graduate. Congregationalist. Officer of Masons and American Legion, member of Improved Order of Redmen and Rotary. Officer of political party. Holder of public office, past and present. Quoted on pp. 80-81, 87, 89, and 96-97.

36 Middle-aged locally-born man of Irish background. Home owner. Graduate training. Member of P.T.A. Roman Catholic. Officer of Knights of Columbus and Exchange Club, member of St. Mary's Holy Name Society, Veterans of World War II, American Legion, and Improved Order of Redmen. Holder of public office, past and present. Quoted on pp. 64, 81, 95, and 97-98.

37 Middle-aged man of Greek background. Local resident for over 20 years. Home owner. Store owner. Less than 8th grade education. Greek Orthodox. Member of Exchange Club.

38 Middle-aged man of German background. Local resident

for over 20 years. Home owner. Factory foreman. 10th grade education. Roman Catholic.

39,40   Middle-aged couple of Italian and English backgrounds respectively. Local residents for less than 5 years. Home owners. Business owners. 10th grade education. Roman Catholics. Quoted on p. 105.

41   Middle-aged man of German background. Local resident for less than 5 years. Home owner. Business owner. College graduate. Quoted on p. 90.

42   Middle-aged man of Italian background. Local resident for over 20 years. Home owner. Store owner. College graduate. Congregationalist. Officer of Rotary and Chamber of Commerce, member of Masons, Ecclesiastical Society, Veterans of World War II, and Pilgrim Brotherhood. Official in Civil Defense organization.

43   Middle-aged woman of English-Irish background. Local resident for over 15 years. Home owner. Business owner. 14th grade education. Member of P.T.A. Roman Catholic. Member of St. Elizabeth's Women's Club. Former holder of public office.

44   Young man of German-English background commuting from out-of-town. Local worker for over 5 years. Store manager. College graduate. Member of Chamber of Commerce.

45   Elderly locally-born man of Irish-English background. Home owner. Business owner. College graduate. Officer of Eastern Pilgrim Head Association.

46   Young locally-born man of Yankee background. Home owner. Owner of realty and insurance company. College graduate. Officer in Congregational Church. Officer of Rotary, Pilgrim Brotherhood, Real Estate Board, and Red Cross Committee, member of Yacht Club and Chamber of Commerce.

47   Middle-aged man of Irish background. Local resident for over 25 years. Home owner. Business manager. 12th grade education. Roman Catholic. Member of Exchange Club. Member of Fire Department.

48   Middle-aged man of Yankee background. Local resident for over 20 years. Home owner. School official. Graduate training. Member of P.T.A. Congregationalist.

49   Middle-aged man of Yankee background. Local resident for over 15 years. School official. Graduate training. Congregationalist. Officer of Rotary, member of American Legion. Quoted on p. 56.

50   Elderly woman of Yankee background. Local resident for over 25 years. Home owner. Owner of realty company and store. Graduate training. Congregationalist. Officer of Green Thumb Club and Weekly Reading Club, member of Musical Society. Quoted on pp. 95 and 97.

51   Elderly locally-born man of Irish background. Officer of bank and lawyer. Graduate training. Roman Catholic. Officer of Knights of Columbus, Rotary, St. Mary's Holy Name Society, and Improved Order of Redmen, member of Chamber of Commerce. Former holder of public office.

52   Young man of Irish background. Local resident for over 20 years. Home owner. Owner of realty and insurance company. College graduate. Roman Catholic. Officer of Chamber of Commerce and Veterans of World War II, member of Exchange Club and Knights of Columbus. Holder of public office. Quoted on pp. 86 and 102.

53   Middle-aged man of Polish background. Local resident for over 40 years. Home owner. 8th grade education. Roman Catholic. Official in Police Department.

54   Middle-aged locally-born man of Irish background. Home owner. Business owner. 13th grade education. Roman Catholic. Member of St. Mary's Holy Name Society, Knights of Columbus, American Legion, and School Board. Former holder of public office. Quoted on pp. 78 and 97.

55   Middle-aged locally-born man of Irish background. Home owner. Lawyer and business man. Graduate training. Roman Catholic. Member of Knights of Columbus, Improved Order of Redmen, St. Mary's Holy Name Society, and Exchange Club. Holder of public office, past and present. Quoted on pp. 39, 88, 92, 96, and 111.

56   Middle-aged man of Russian background. Local resident for over 30 years. Home owner. Business owner. 11th grade education. Jewish. Officer of Exchange Club.

Member of Chamber of Commerce, American Legion, Veterans of World War II, and Yacht Club. Official in Police Department and member of Fire Department.

57 Middle-aged woman of English background. Local resident for over 20 years. Home owner. Graduate training. Episcopalian. Officer of Women's Republican Club, member of School Board and Apple Valley Country Club. Quoted on pp. 48, 80, and 99.

58 Young locally-born man of Polish background. Home owner. Union official. 12th grade education. Roman Catholic. Officer of P.T.A. Member of Improved Order of Redmen, Knights of Columbus, and St. Mary's Holy Name Society. Official in Police Department.

59 Middle-aged locally-born man of Yankee background. Home owner. Store owner. College graduate. Officer of Baptist Church and Baptist Men's Brotherhood.

60 Middle-aged man of Irish background. Local resident for over 10 years. Home owner. Owner of realty and insurance company. 10th grade education. Roman Catholic. Officer of Chamber of Commerce, Grange, and Exchange Club. Former holder of public office. Quoted on pp. 44 and 98.

61 Middle-aged man of Italian background. Local resident for over 35 years. Home owner. Tavern owner. Less than 8th grade education. Roman Catholic. Member of Knights of Columbus, St. Mary's Holy Name Society, and Gun Club. Former member of Fire Department.

62 Elderly man of Yankee background. Local resident for over 50 years. Home owner. Factory owner and official of realty company. 12th grade education. Officer in Congregational Church. Officer of Rotary, member of Pilgrim Brotherhood. Former holder of public office.

63 Elderly locally-born man of Irish background. Home owner. Owner of realty and insurance company and bank official. 10th grade education. Officer in Episcopalian Church. Officer of Republican Club. Member of Masons. Holder of public office. Quoted on p. 82.

64 Middle-aged locally-born man of Irish background. Official in bank and post office. 12th grade education.

Roman Catholic. Officer of Veterans of Foreign Wars and American Legion. Member of School Board.

65   Middle-aged man of Yankee background. Local resident for over 15 years. Home owner. Owner of construction company. 9th grade education. Episcopalian. Officer of Improved Order of Redmen, member of Exchange Club and Masons. Former holder of public office and member of Fire Department. Quoted on p. 122.

66   Elderly man of Russian background. Local resident for over 50 years. Home owner. Official of bank, realty company, and hotel. Graduate training. Jewish. Officer of Chamber of Commerce, member of Masons, Improved Order of Redmen, and School Board. Former holder of public office. Quoted on pp. 42-43, 44, 52, 53, 66, and 104.

67   Middle-aged locally-born woman of Irish background. Home owner. Schoolteacher. 14th grade education. Roman Catholic. Member of Teachers' League and St. Mary's Guild.

68   Young man of Italian background. Local resident for over 15 years. Store owner. Less than 8th grade education. Roman Catholic. Officer of Italian-American Club, member of Florentine Society, Chamber of Commerce, and Grange.

69   Middle-aged locally-born man of Yugoslavian background. Home owner. Factory foreman and bank official. 8th grade education. Roman Catholic. Officer of Community Council, Knights of Columbus, St. Mary's Holy Name Society, and Boy Scouts. Former official of Fire Department. Quoted on p. 84.

70   Middle-aged locally-born man of Yankee background. Home owner. Store owner. 10th grade education. Protestant. Former holder of public office and official in Police Department.

71   Middle-aged man of Swedish background. Local resident for over 35 years. Home owner. Factory foreman and union official. 14th grade education. Officer in Baptist Church. Member of Swedish Lodge and Baptist Men's Brotherhood. Quoted on pp. 82, 98, and 104.

72   Elderly locally-born man of English background. Home owner. Store owner. 14th grade education. Officer in

Episcopalian Church. Officer of Masons. Former holder of public office. Quoted on pp. 63 and 67.

73 Middle-aged locally-born woman of Yankee background. Home owner. Professional woman. 14th grade education. Official in Congregational Church. Officer of P.T.A. and Congregational Social Workers. Member of Green Thumb Club.

74 Middle-aged woman of Hungarian background. Local resident for over 10 years. 15th grade education. Officer in Congregational Church. Officer of P.T.A., Platonians, and Congregational Women's Club.

75 Middle-aged man of Yankee background commuting from out-of-town. Local worker for less than 5 years. Home owner. Bank official. 14th grade education. Member of Pilgrim Brotherhood and Trinity Fellowship. Quoted on p. 85.

76 Middle-aged man of Yankee background. Local resident for over 50 years. Home owner. Store owner. 11th grade education. Officer of Improved Order of Redmen, member of Masons and Republican Club. Former member of Fire Department. Quoted on pp. 70-71.

77 Young man of Scotch-English background. Local resident for less than 5 years. Home owner. Professional man. Graduate training. Congregationalist. Member of P.T.A. Quoted on p. 53.

78 Elderly woman of English background. Local resident for over 65 years. Home owner. 11th grade education. Official in Congregational Church. Officer of W.C.T.U., member of P.T.A., Weekly Reading Club, and Musical Society. Quoted on pp. 27, 93, and 109.

79 Young locally-born man of Swedish background. Home owner. Skilled worker. 14th grade education. Officer in Baptist Church. Officer of Baptist Brotherhood and Andante Club, member of Masons, Gun Club, and Musical Society. Quoted on p. 116.

80 Middle-aged man of Italian background. Local resident for over 40 years. Home owner. Factory foreman. 10th grade education. Baptist. Officer of Italian-American Club, Veterans of World War II, Disabled American Veterans, Republican Club, and Baptist Men's Brother-

hood, member of Gun Club, Improved Order of Redmen, and Pilgrim Brotherhood. Holder of public office, past and present.

81,82   Middle-aged couple of Yankee background. Local residents for over 25 years. Husband factory worker. 11th grade education. Baptists. Husband officer of American Legion. Wife officer of American Legion Auxiliary and Welfare League, and member of Red Cross. Quoted on p. 105.

83   Elderly woman of Yankee background. Local resident for over 20 years. 13th grade education. Officer of Congregational Church. Officer of Visiting Nurse Association and Pleasant Society, member of Green Thumb Club and Apple Valley Country Club. Quoted on p. 87.

84   Middle-aged man of Italian background. Local resident for over 35 years. Factory worker. Union official. 10th grade education. Roman Catholic. Member of Florentine Society. Quoted on pp. 64, 93-94, and 115.

85   Young man of Irish background. Local resident for over 5 years. Store owner out-of-town. 13th grade education. Roman Catholic. Officer of St. Mary's Holy Name Society, member of Knights of Columbus, Veterans of World War II, and Young Republican Club. Official in Police Department.

86   Elderly locally-born woman of Yankee background. Former hotel owner. 8th grade education. Officer of Baptist Church. Officer of Welfare League and Women's Relief Corps, member of Missionary Society and Republican Club. Quoted on p. 87.

87   Middle-aged man of Yankee background. Local resident for over 20 years. Store owner and bank official. 8th grade education. Congregationalist. Officer of Republican Club, member of Yacht Club. Former holder of public office. Quoted on pp. 50-51 and 66.

88   Young man of Scotch background. Local resident for over 30 years. Home owner. White-collar worker. 12th grade education. Officer of Congregational Church. Officer of Pilgrim Brotherhood and Republican Club, member of Ecclesiastical Society and Young Republican Club. Official in Police Department.

89   Elderly woman of English background. Local resident
      for over 60 years. Home owner. 8th grade education.
      Officer of Baptist Church. Officer of Visiting Nurse
      Association, Missionary Society and Welfare League,
      member of Weekly Reading Club and Republican Town
      Committee.

90   Young woman of Italian background commuting from
      out-of-town. Local worker for over 10 years. Home owner.
      Store owner. 12th grade education. Officer of Chamber
      of Commerce. Quoted on pp. 69 and 104.

91   Middle-aged man of Yankee background. Local resident
      for over 20 years. Home owner. Professional man. Grad-
      uate training. Jewish. Member of Masons. Quoted on pp.
      82-83.

92   Middle-aged locally-born man of Swedish background.
      Home owner. Business owner and official of realty
      companies and banks. 8th grade education. Congrega-
      tionalist. Officer of Republican Club, Rotary, and
      American Legion, member of Improved Order of Red-
      men, Swedish Lodge, Pilgrim Brotherhood, Yacht Club,
      and Apple Valley Country Club. Former holder of
      public office and official of Fire Department and Police
      Department. Quoted on pp. 69, 87-88, and 96.

93   Young locally-born man of Yankee background. Home
      owner. Factory official. College graduate. Officer of
      Congregational Church. Officer of Pilgrim Brotherhood,
      member of P.T.A., Republican Club, and Apple Valley
      Country Club. Quoted on pp. 35, 52, 88, 89, 96, 97, 107,
      and 115.

94   Middle-aged man of German background. Local resident
      for over 20 years. Home owner. Manager of factory.
      College graduate. Officer of Congregational Church.
      Officer of Ecclesiastical Society, Boy Scouts, and De
      Molay (Masons), member of School Board, Pilgrim Broth-
      erhood, Chamber of Commerce, and Masons. Former
      holder of public office. Quoted on pp. 46, 79, 88, 99,
      107, and 116.

95   Middle-aged locally-born woman of Yankee background.
      Home owner. Professional woman. College graduate.
      Officer in Congregational Church. Officer of Visiting

Nurse Association, Red Cross, Girl Scouts, Junior Musical Society, and Pleasant Society. Quoted on pp. 28, 35, 36, and 86.

96,97   Middle-aged couple of Irish background. Local residents for over 10 years. Husband factory worker and union official. Less than 8th grade education. Roman Catholics. Husband officer of Knights of Columbus and St. Mary's Holy Name Society, member of Democratic Town Committee, and former holder of public office. Wife officer of P.T.A. and Women's Democratic Club, member of Ladies Guild. Quoted on p. 103.

98   Elderly woman of Yankee background. Local resident for over 35 years. 14th grade education. Baptist. Officer of Visiting Nurse Association, Red Cross, Junior Musical Society and Andante Club, member of Weekly Reading Club. Quoted on pp. 65 and 90-91.

99   Middle-aged woman of Yankee background. Local resident for over 30 years. Home owner. 12th grade education. Episcopalian. Officer of Visiting Nurse Association, League of Women Voters, Green Thumb Club, Weekly Reading Club, and Women's Republican Club, member of P.T.A., Rector's Aide, Trinity Guild, and Republican Town Committee. Quoted on p. 98.

100   Elderly locally-born man of Yankee background. Home owner. Business owner. 8th grade education. Baptist. Member of Masons, Yacht Club, Gun Club, and Republican Town Committee. Former official in Fire Department.

101   Middle-aged man of English background. Local resident for over 15 years. Home owner. Professional man and bank official. Graduate training. Congregationalist. Member of Apple Valley Country Club. Quoted on p. 73.

102   Middle-aged man of Yankee background. Local resident for over 15 years. Home owner. Professional man. Graduate training. Baptist. Former holder of public office. Quoted on p. 100.

103   Middle-aged woman of Yankee background. Local resident for over 15 years. Professional woman. Graduate training. Quoted on p. 66.

104 Middle-aged locally-born woman of Yankee background. Home owner. College graduate. Baptist. Member of Weekly Reading Club and Green Thumb Club. Quoted on p. 64.

105 Central City real estate man with holdings in Connecticut Town. Quoted on p. 45.

Appendix C

A. Residence

1. Realty and insurance companies
   - a. Owners 6
   - b. Officers 4
2. Real Estate Board
   - a. Officers 1
3. Land Development Associations
   - a. Officers 3

B. Occupation

1. Banks
   - a. Officers 16
2. Insurance companies
   - a. Members 5
3. Factories
   - a. Officers 3
   - b. Managers 1
   - c. Foremen 2
   - d. Workers 5
   - e. Union officials 5
   - f. Union members .. 5
4. Professional 7
5. Stores
   - a. Owners 29
   - b. Managers 4
6. Shops
   - a. Owners 5
7. Businesses
   - a. Owners 21
   - b. Managers 3
   - c. Salesmen 1

C. School

1. P.T.A.
   - a. Officers 5
   - b. Members 8
2. School Board 6
3. Teachers' League 1
4. School Officials 3

D. Social and Religious
Church

1. Episcopal
   - a. Officers 2
   - b. Members 8
   - c. Rector's Aide Members 1
   - d. Trinity Fellowship Members 1
   - e. Trinity Guild Members 1
2. Congregational
   - a. Officers 13
   - b. Members 12
   - c. Pilgrim Brotherhood
     - Officers 3
     - Members 9
   - d. Ecclesiastical Society
     - Officers 1
     - Members 2
   - e. Social Workers
     - Officers 1
   - f. Missionary Society
     - Officers 2
     - Members 1
   - g. Women's Club
     - Officers 1
   - h. Platonians
     - Officers 1
   - i. Pleasant Society
     - Officers 2
3. Baptist
   - a. Officers 5
   - b. Members 6

161

c. Baptist Men's Brotherhood
Officers 3
Members 1
d. Welfare League
Officers 3
4. Lutheran
a. Officers 1
5. Catholic
a. Officers 1
b. Members 36
c. St. Mary's Holy Name Society
Officers 4
Members 7
d. St. Mary's Ladies Guild
Members 2
e. Knights of Columbus
Officers 5
Members 8
f. St. Elizabeth's Women's Club
Members 1
g. St. Elizabeth's Men's Club
Members 1
6. Jewish
a. Members 9
7. Greek Orthodox
a. Members 1
8. No Church 8
9. Christian Endeavor Society
a. Officers 1

Nonchurch

1. Rotary
a. Officers 12
b. Members 4
2. Chamber of Commerce
a. Officers 6
b. Members 17
3. Exchange Club
a. Officers 3
b. Members 8
4. Grange
a. Officers 2
b. Members 2
5. Restaurant Guild
a. Members 1

6. American Legion
a. Officers 5
b. Members 6
7. American Legion Auxiliary
a. Officers 1
8. Veterans of World War II
a. Officers 2
b. Members 6
9. Disabled American Veterans
a. Officers 1
b. Members 1
10. Veterans of Foreign Wars
a. Officers 1
11. Masons
a. Officers 3
b. Members 14
12. De Molay (Masons)
a. Officers 1
13. Improved Order of Redmen
a. Officers 3
b. Members 7
14. Gun Club
a. Members 7
15. Yacht Club
a. Members 5
16. Green Thumb Club
a. Officers 2
b. Members 2
17. Weekly Reading Club
a. Officers 2
b. Members 3
18. Apple Valley Country Club
a. Members 5
19. Swedish Lodge
a. Members 2
20. Boy Scouts
a. Officers 2
b. Members 1
21. Girl Scouts
a. Officers 1
b. Members 1
22. Musical Society
a. Officers 1
b. Members 3
23. Junior Musical Society
a. Officers 2

24. Andante Club
    a. Officers 2
25. Women's Relief Corps
    a. Officers 1
26. W.C.T.U.
    a. Officers 1
27. Italian-American Club
    a. Officers 4
28. Florentine Society
    a. Members 2
29. Croatian Fraternal Union
    a. Members 1
30. Visiting Nurse Association
    a. Officers 5
31. American Red Cross
    a. Officers 3
    b. Members 1

E. Politics

1. Republican Club
   a. Officers 4
   b. Members 4
2. Young Republican Club
   a. Officers 1
   b. Members 2
3. Women's Republican Club
   a. Officers 2
4. Republican Town Meeting
   Committee
   a. Members 4
5. Democratic Club
   a. Officers 1
6. Women's Democratic Club
   a. Officers 1
7. Democratic Town Meeting
   Committee
   a. Officers 1
   b. Members 1
8. League of Women Voters
   a. Officers 1
9. Chairmen of Taxpayers
   Party (Independent) .. 1
10. Selectmen 4
11. Councilmen 2
12. Town Clerk 1

13. Town Treasurer 2
14. Town Assessor 4
15. Board of Finance
    a. Officers 2
    b. Members 1
16. Chairman of Rationing
    Board 1
17. Head of Civil Defense .. 1
18. Park Commissioner 1
19. Irving Field Committee
    a. Members 1
20. Mosquito Control Com-
    mittee
    a. Members 1
21. Tree Warden 1
22. Dog Warden 1
23. Probation Officer 1
24. Burgess 1
25. Warden of Borough 2
26. Community Council
    a. Officers 2
27. Recreation Advisory Board
    a. Members 1
28. Library Clerk 1
29. State Legislature
    Representatives 4
30. Police Commissioner 6
31. Police Department
    a. Officers 1
32. Auxiliary Police, Civil
    Defense 1
33. Fire Department
    a. Officers 3
    b. Members 6
34. Post Office
    a. Officers 1
    b. Members 1
35. Judge of Town Court .. 2
36. Deputy Judge, Town
    Court 2
37. Justice of the Peace 1
38. Judge of Probate Court 1
39. Prosecuting Attorney .. 1
40. Asst. Prosecuting Att'y 1
41. Apple Valley Association
    a. Officers 1

Notes

Notes

CHAPTER ONE

Introduction

1. See Allison Davis, Burleigh B. Gardner, and Mary R. Gardner, *Deep South* (Chicago: The University of Chicago Press, 1941); Hortense Powder-maker, *After Freedom: A Cultural Study in the Deep South* (New York: The Viking Press, 1939); John Dollard, *Caste and Class in a Southern Town* (New Haven: Yale University Press, 1937); Bertram Wilbur Doyle, *The Etiquette of Race Relations in the South* (Chicago: The University of Chicago Press, 1937); among others.

Also see some of the studies on the personality development of Negro youth in various parts of the South and near South prepared for the American Youth Commission: Allison Davis and John Dollard, *Children of Bondage* (Washington, D.C.: American Council on Education, 1940); E. Franklin Frazier, *Negro Youth at the Crossways* (Washington, D.C.: American Council on Education, 1940); Charles S. Johnson, *Growing Up in the Black Belt* (Washington, D.C.: American Council on Education, 1941); J. Howell Atwood *et al., Thus Be Their Destiny* (Washington, D.C.: American Council on Education, 1941).

2. See St. Clair Drake and Horace R. Cayton, *Black Metropolis* (New York: Harcourt, Brace and Co., 1945); Robert Austin Warner, *New Haven Negroes* (New Haven: Yale University Press, 1940); Clara A. Hardin, *The Negroes of Philadelphia* (Published Ph.D. dissertation, Bryn Mawr College, 1945); Robert C. Weaver, *The Negro Ghetto* (New York: Harcourt, Brace and Co., 1948); among others.

3. See Gunnar Myrdal, *An American Dilemma* (New York: Harper and Bros., 1944); E. Franklin Frazier, *The Negro in the United States* (rev. ed.; New York: The Macmillan Co., 1957); Maurice R. Davie, *Negroes in American Society* (New York: McGraw-Hill Book Co., 1949); Charles S. Johnson, *Patterns of Negro Segregation* (New York: Harper and Bros., 1943).

4. For two of the few examples of narrowly delimited studies of small Northern towns, see Arthur Katona, "A Survey of Discrimination in a Northern Town," *Social Forces,* Vol. 26, No. 4, May 1948, pp. 443-450; and Thomas C. McCormick and Richard A. Hornseth, "The Negro in Madison, Wisconsin," *American Sociological Review,* Vol. 12, No. 5, October 1947, pp. 519-525.

5. Myrdal, *op. cit.,* pp. 60-67, 587-588, has suggested a rank order of discriminations in terms of white and Negro values. Johnson, *Patterns of Negro Segregation,* pp. 3-155, 173-185, has also mentioned the existence of such a pattern of race relations.

6. See Edward Alsworth Ross, *Social Control* (New York: The Macmillan Co., 1901); Frederick E. Lumley, *Means of Social Control* (New York: The

Century Co., 1925) ; Luther L. Bernard, *Social Control in its Sociological Aspects* (New York: The Macmillan Co., 1939); Carl A. Dawson and Warner E. Gettys, *An Introduction to Sociology* (New York: The Ronald Press Co., 1929) ; John Lewis Gillin and John Philip Gillin, *Cultural Sociology* (rev. ed.; New York: The Macmillan Co., 1948) ; and Richard T. LaPiere, *A Theory of Social Control* (New York: McGraw-Hill Book Co., 1954) ; among others.

7. See Charles H. Cooley, *Human Nature and the Social Order* (New York: C. Scribner's Sons, 1902) ; Paul H. Landis, *Social Control* (rev. ed.; Chicago: J. B. Lippincott Co., 1956) ; Ellsworth Faris, *The Nature of Human Nature* (New York: McGraw-Hill Book Co., 1937); Edwin M. Lemert, "The Folkways and Social Control," *American Sociological Review*, Vol. 7, No. 3, June 1942, pp. 394-399, and "The Grand Jury as an Agency of Social Control," *American Sociological Review*, Vol. 10, No. 6, December 1945, pp. 751-758; and Frank Hamilton Hankins, *An Introduction to the Study of Society* (New York: The Macmillan Co., 1930) ; among others.

8. See William Graham Sumner, *Folkways* (Boston: Ginn and Co., 1906) ; A. B. Hollingshead, "The Concept of Social Control," *American Sociological Review*, Vol. 6, No. 2, April 1941, pp. 217-224; J. O. Hertzler, *Social Institutions* (Lincoln, Neb.: University of Nebraska Press, 1946); E. B. Reuter and C. W. Hart, *Introduction to Sociology* (New York: McGraw-Hill Book Co., 1933) ; Raymond Firth, *Elements of Social Organization* (New York: Philosophical Library, 1951) ; and A. R. Radcliffe-Brown, "Sanctions, Social," *Encyclopaedia of the Social Sciences*, Vol. 13, pp. 531-534 (New York: The Macmillan Co., 1937) ; among others.

9. George C. Homans, *The Human Group* (New York: Harcourt, Brace and Co., 1950) , and LaPiere, *op. cit.*, are outstanding among those who stress the importance of the group as a setting for social control.

10. U. S. Bureau of the Census, *U. S. Census of Population: 1950*, Vol. 1, Number of Inhabitants, Chapter 7: Connecticut.

11. This description is taken from C. Wendell King, "Branford Center: A Community Study in Social Cleavage" (Unpublished Ph.D. dissertation, Yale University, 1943) , pp. 7-12. Aside from the number of inhabitants, the 1950 census material did not reveal any significant changes in the composition of the population as reported above.

12. Dollard, *op. cit.*, p. 17.

CHAPTER TWO

Background of Race Relations in Connecticut Town

1. Almon Wheeler Lauber, *Indian Slavery in Colonial Times Within the Present Limits of the United States* (New York: Columbia University, 1913), *Studies in History, Economics and Public Law*, Vol. 54, No. 3, edited by the Faculty of Political Science of Columbia University, pp. 109-111, 122-130.

2. Lorenzo Johnston Greene, *The Negro in Colonial New England, 1620-1776* (New York: Columbia University Press, 1942) , pp. 15-18.

3. Bernard C. Steiner, *History of Slavery in Connecticut* (Baltimore: The Johns Hopkins Press, 1893), *Johns Hopkins University Studies in Historical and Political Science,* Herbert B. Adams, ed., Eleventh Series, IX-X, p. 23n.

4. Frederick Calvin Norton, "Negro Slavery in Connecticut," *The Connecticut Magazine,* Vol. V, No. 6, June 1899, p. 320.

5. Greene, *op. cit.,* p. 23.

6. *Ibid.,* pp. 126-129, 132, 312-313; Steiner, *op. cit.,* p. 13.

7. Greene, *op. cit.,* p. 282.

8. *Ibid.,* p. 218 ff.

9. Mary Hewitt Mitchell, *History of New Haven County, Connecticut,* Vol. 1 (Chicago: The Pioneer Historical Publishing Co., 1930), pp. 417-419.

10. *The Public Statutes (and) Laws of the State of Connecticut as Revised in May 1821* (1821), p. 430. Quoted in Greene, *op. cit.,* p. 66.

11. Greene, *op. cit.,* pp. 187-188.

12. *Ibid.,* pp. 73-74, 89-90.

13. *Ibid.,* p. 74.

14. Mitchell, *op. cit.,* p. 419.

15. Greene, *op. cit.,* pp. 76-77.

16. *Ibid.,* pp. 76, 89.

17. *Ibid.,* p. 47.

18. John C. Carr, *Old Branford,* Branford, Conn.: The Branford Printing Co., [1935?], p. 47.

19. Greene, *op. cit.,* p. 345.

20. Rev. Elijah C. Baldwin, [Miscellaneous Comments on Branford], *The Home World,* Vol. 2, No. 11 (1888), p. 675.

21. *Branford Land Records,* Vol. 22, p. k.

22. U. S. Bureau of the Census, *Thirteenth Census of the United States: 1910 Population,* Vol. II (Washington: Government Printing Office, 1913), p. 260.

23. U. S. Bureau of the Census, *Fourteenth Census of the United States: 1920 Population,* Vol. II (Washington: Government Printing Office, 1922), p. 160.

24. U. S. Bureau of the Census, *Fifteenth Census of the United States: 1930 Population,* Vol. III, Part 1 (Washington: Government Printing Office, 1932), p. 364.

25. Cf. Thomas C. McCormick and Richard A. Hornseth, "The Negro in Madison, Wisconsin," *American Sociological Review,* Vol. 12, No. 5, October 1947, pp. 519-525, where the same characteristic of a transient Negro population is mentioned.

CHAPTER THREE

Race Relations in Connecticut Town, 1950-1952.

1. This and other aspects of Negro housing, which are discussed on this and the following page, are essentially the same for Negroes elsewhere in the United States. Cf. J. Howell Atwood *et al., Thus Be Their Destiny*

(Washington, D. C.: American Council on Education, 1941), pp. 1-3, 8-13, 68-70. Also see Gunnar Myrdal, *An American Dilemma* (New York: Harper and Bros., 1944), pp. 376-379, 621, 1125-1128; Robert C. Weaver, *The Negro Ghetto* (New York: Harcourt, Brace and Co., 1948), pp. 66-68; Maurice R. Davie, *Negroes in American Society* (New York: McGraw-Hill Book Co., 1949), pp. 218-221; Roi Ottley, *'New World A-Coming'* (New York: Literary Classics, Inc., 1943), pp. 154-155; The National Urban League, *A Review of the Social and Economic Conditions of the Negro Population of Hartford, Connecticut* (New York: September-October, 1944), pp. 27-29.

2. This has been the case since 1948 when the Supreme Court ruled that agreements made by property owners not to sell to Negroes were legally unenforceable. See George Eaton Simpson and J. Milton Yinger, *Racial and Cultural Minorities* (New York: Harper and Bros., 1953), pp. 444-447, for a more detailed analysis of restrictive convenants and this historic decision.

3. See Charles S. Johnson, *The Negro in American Civilization* (New York: Henry Holt and Co., 1930), pp. 92-93, for a discussion of industrial housing for Negro workers.

4. For a thorough refutation of this argument, see Robert C. Weaver, *The Negro Ghetto* (New York: Harcourt, Brace and Co., 1948), pp. 279-303; and Charles Abrams, *Forbidden Neighbors: A Study of Prejudice in Housing* (New York: Harper and Bros., 1955), pp. 164-168, 279-292.

5. The general pattern of Negro occupational categories in Connecticut Town as described in the following pages follows closely that of the United States as a whole. It is, of course, influenced by local conditions and facts, i.e., the almost complete absence of a professional class. See the National Urban League, *op. cit.*, pp. 9-11, 15-19; Ira DeA. Reid, *In a Minor Key: Negro Youth in Story and Fact* (Washington, D. C.: American Council on Education, 1940), p. 63; Atwood *et al.*, *op. cit.*, pp. 13-14, 67-68, 87-89; Davie, *op. cit.*, pp. 107-108, 110-114, 125, 130-131; E. Franklin Frazier, *The Negro in the United States* (New York: The Macmillan Co., 1949), pp. 234-235, 240-241, 249-250, 254-256, 267-272; Myrdal, *op. cit.*, pp. 294, 296-297, 380, 388-395, 1082-1087, 1115-1119; St. Clair Drake and Horace R. Cayton, *Black Metropolis* (New York: Harcourt, Brace and Co., 1945), pp. 112, 214-235, 242-252.

6. See Charles S. Johnson, *Growing Up in the Black Belt* (Washington, D. C.: American Council on Education, 1941), pp. 193-194. For mention of the lack of skilled or trained Negro workers, see also Charles S. Johnson and associates, *To Stem This Tide: A Survey of Racial Tension Areas in the United States* (Boston: The Pilgrim Press, 1943), pp. 3, 14-15, 121; Edwin R. Embree, *Brown Americans* (New York: The Viking Press, 1944), p. 120; Charles S. Johnson and associates, *Into the Main Stream: A Survey of Best Practices in Race Relations in the South* (Chapel Hill: The University of North Carolina Press, 1947), p. 112.

7. For a more detailed discussion of labor and union attitudes toward Negroes, see Henry Lee Moon, *Balance of Power: The Negro Vote* (Garden City, New York: Doubleday and Co., Inc., 1948), pp. 132 ff.; The National Urban League, *op. cit.*, pp. 23-24; Embree, *op. cit.*, pp. 122-126; Herbert R. Northrup, "Discrimination and the Trade Unions," *Discrimination and National Welfare*, ed. by R. M. MacIver (New York: Institute for Religious

and Social Studies, 1949), pp. 65-69, 75-76; Johnson, *To Stem This Tide*, pp. 7-8, 15-16, 20-21.

8. For a more detailed presentation of the possible effectiveness of this type of law, see Malcolm Ross, *All Manner of Men* (New York: Reynal and Hitchcock, 1948), pp. 49-169.

9. How unusual and "advanced" this situation is in many instances can be seen by reference to the situation in other Northern schools. Cf. Atwood *et al.*, *op. cit.*, pp. 5, 72; and Henry T. Bourne, Jr., "Young and Colored: A Study of the Educational Ideals and Problems of Negro School Children in New Haven" (Unpublished Senior Essay, Yale Sociology Department, 1949), p. 101.

10. Cf. Atwood *et al.*, *op. cit.*, p. 5, for confirmation of this general situation in other similar Northern towns.

11. The same lack of encouragement for Negro school children by school authorities has been noted elsewhere. See Johnson, *To Stem This Tide*, p. 4; Drake and Cayton, *op. cit.*, p. 259; Ottley, *op. cit.*, p. 161; Bourne, *op. cit.*, p. 33.

12. This award contrasts with certain discriminatory attitudes held by the D.A.R. elsewhere, for which see Davie, *op. cit*, p. 302.

13. See Oliver Cromwell Cox, *Caste, Class, and Race* (Garden City, New York: Doubleday and Co., 1948), pp. 290, 346; Johnson, *Into the Main Stream*, pp. 281-282, 286-293; Myrdal, *op. cit.*, pp. 868-872, for more detailed comments on segregated churches. Also see Myrdal, *op. cit.*, p. 601, where he mentions Negroes as attending white churches in "several minor cities in New England with a small stable Negro population." This is not the case in Connecticut Town.

14. For a statement of the Roman Catholic Church's increasingly liberal position on the race question as it affects the church itself, see Johnson, *Into the Main Stream*, pp. 283-284. Also see John LaFarge, *The Race Question and the Negro* (New York: Longmans, Green and Co., 1943). This trend has intensified still more in recent years, particularly in the South.

15. See Charles S. Johnson, *Patterns of Negro Segregation* (New York: Harper and Bros., 1943), p. 146; Davie, *op. cit.*, p. 178, for the effect of residential segregation on other activities and areas of behavior.

16. See Atwood *el al.*, *op. cit.*, p. 79, for a description of a different situation.

17. See Davie, *op. cit.*, pp. 299-300, for a summary statement of discriminatory racial policies followed by various semipublic white national organizations, branches of some of which are found in Connecticut Town.

18. It might be mentioned that in at least one other nearby small Connecticut town with a population of around 5,000, the American Legion Post elected a Negro as its commander in the early fifties. He is the only Negro member of the Post in town.

19. Contrast this with the situation in Hartford where Negroes have worked in both organizations. See The National Urban League, *op. cit.*, pp. 60-61.

20. For contrast see Johnson, *Into the Main Stream*, pp. 52-53, for a list of Southern cities employing Negro policemen as compiled from *Southern Frontier*, Report of the Greater Little Rock Urban League, and from field reports. Also see "Changing Patterns in the New South," by the Southern

Regional Council, Vols. 9 and 10, December-January, 1954-1955, p. 35, for the number of Negro police in the South. As for the North, see the National Urban League, *op. cit.*, pp. 13-14, for the situation in Hartford as it affects both the Police and Fire Departments. Central City has Negro policemen, but no Negro firemen.

21. By and large, these facts, especially those relating to Negro crime, are contrary to those reported elsewhere in the United States. This is true even for the North. See The National Urban League, *op. cit.*, pp. 45-47; John G. Van Deusen, *The Black Man in White America*, (rev. ed.; Washington, D. C.: Associated Publishers, Inc., 1944), pp. 142-157; Davie, *op. cit.*, pp. 251-261; Embree, *op. cit.*, pp. 166-168; Myrdal, *op. cit.*, pp. 526-529, 966-979; Atwood *et al., op. cit.*, p. 78. However, cf. Atwood *et al., op. cit.*, p. 2, for a similar situation in a town of comparable size and composition.

22. Again the local situation differs from that found in other Northern cities. See Embree, *op. cit.*, pp. 137-138; Atwood *et al., op. cit.*, p. 2.

23. Negroes in Connecticut Town appear to be less active politically than those in other Northern cities. See Davie, *op. cit.*, pp. 279-282; Myrdal, *op. cit.*, pp. 437-440, 491-493.

24. This seems to have been true everywhere of Northern Negro voters. See Drake and Cayton, *op. cit.*, pp. 109, 209-210; Moon, *op. cit.*, pp. 18-19; Myrdal, *op. cit.*, pp. 493-495.

25. Cf. Atwood *et al., op. cit.*, p. 5, where he reports public facilities in Milton, Penna., as being less discriminatory.

26. See Myrdal, *op. cit.*, p. 637, for a similar statement.

27. See below, p. 71. Also see Johnson, *Patterns of Negro Segregation*, p. 145, where greater discrimination is reported in restaurants than in bars and taverns.

28. Those operated by state or local authorities are nondiscriminatory. Also see Myrdal, *op. cit.*, pp. 617, 634, where he mentions discrimination in the North against Negro use of privately and publicly operated bathing facilities.

29. The clothing and department store situation in Connecticut Town appears to be better than that reported elsewhere by other authorities. See Atwood *et al., op. cit.*, p. 87; Myrdal, *op. cit.*, p. 637.

30. Restaurant discrimination was referred to above. Also see Myrdal, *op. cit.*, pp. 528, 609; Johnson, *Patterns of Negro Segregation*, p. 59.

31. The availability of overnight accommodations for Negroes is pretty much the same as elsewhere in the North. See Drake and Cayton, *op. cit.*, pp. 107-108; Atwood *et al., op. cit.*, pp. 5, 80.

32. See Davie, *op. cit.*, p. 291; Myrdal, *op. cit.*, p. 630, for remarks on the general lack of effectiveness of this type of law.

33. See Myrdal, *op. cit.*, pp. 60-67, 587-588.

34. See W. S. M. Banks, II, "The Rank Order of Sensitivity to Discriminations of Negroes in Columbus, Ohio," *American Sociological Review*, Vol. 15, No. 4, August 1950, pp. 529-534.

35. See Edwin R. Edmunds, "The Myrdalian Thesis: Rank Order of Discrimination," *Phylon*, Vol. 15, No. 3, September 1954, pp. 297-303.

CHAPTER FOUR

Processes and Techniques of Control

1. For further references to the Negro's low socioeconomic status and how it helps to set him apart from the rest of society, see Gunnar Myrdal, *An American Dilemma* (New York: Harper and Bros., 1944), pp. 75-78, 491, 602, 652.

2. See Charles S. Johnson and associates, *Into the Main Stream: A Survey of Best Practices in Race Relations in the South* (Chapel Hill: The University of North Carolina, 1947), p. 112; Robert C. Weaver, *The Negro Ghetto* (New York: Harcourt, Brace and Co., 1948), pp. 27-28; Myrdal *op. cit.*, pp. 390-391; Maurice R. Davie, *Negroes in American Society* (New York: McGraw-Hill Book Co., 1949), pp. 128-129, for further analysis of a low development of Negro education and training and some of its ramifications.

3. See Robert C. Weaver, "Effect on Housing," *Discrimination and National Welfare*, ed. R. M. MacIver (New York: Institute for Religious and Social Studies, 1949), p. 25; Myrdal, *op. cit.*, pp. 205-208, for reference to poverty and some of its results as far as maintenance of the race relations pattern is concerned.

4. Allison Davis, "The Motivation of the Underprivileged Worker," *Industry and Society*, ed. William Foote Whyte (New York: McGraw-Hill Book Co., 1946), pp. 84-106, brilliantly brings out some of the cultural and socioeconomic factors which help to strengthen this irresponsible behavior of any underprivileged worker. He points out that the industrial virtues of promptness and dependability are not touched upon in the socialization of the underprivileged worker because in this situation there has been no opportunity for these motives to become rewarding.

5. Cf. John S. Ellsworth, Jr., *Factory Folkways* (New Haven: Yale University Press, 1952), pp. 150-151, 188; Oliver Cromwell Cox, *Caste, Class, and Race* (New York: Doubleday and Co., 1948), pp. 354-355; Myrdal, *op. cit.*, pp. 386-387; Weaver, *The Negro Ghetto*, p. 29, for more details on how the presence of nonlocal Negroes (or other strangers) adversely affects the race situation.

6. For examples of the effect of large and rapid increases of strangers or out-groupers, i.e., Negroes, on race relations, see St. Clair Drake and Horace R. Cayton, *Black Metropolis* (New York: Harcourt, Brace and Co., 1945), pp. 73-76, 177; Myrdal, *op. cit.*, pp. 167-168, 601. Also see H. M. Blalock, "Economic Discrimination and Negro Increase," *American Sociological Review*, Vol. 21, No. 5, October 1956, pp. 584-588, where he does a needed job of qualifying this over-all generalization.

7. For a definition of the mores and examples of them in operation, see William Graham Sumner, *Folkways* (Boston: Ginn and Co., 1906), pp. 2-4, 30-31; Charles S. Johnson, *To Stem This Tide: A Survey of Racial Tension Areas in the United States* (Boston: The Pilgrim Press, 1943), p. 40; Charles S. Johnson, *Patterns of Negro Segregation* (New York: Harper and Bros., 1943), p. 200; Myrdal, *op. cit.*, pp. 20, 525, 831, 1031-1032, 1048-1049, 1053-1054; Cox, *op. cit.*, pp. 468-473.

8. See Davie, *op. cit.*, pp. 364-367, 383, 475, 488; Myrdal, *op. cit.*, pp.

30-32, 88-89, 103-108, 208, 215-219, 283-284, 575, 582-585, 603, 1027-1031, for examples and discussion of rationalizations in race relations.

9. As an illustration of the lack of validity for this rationalization, see E. F. Schietinger, "Racial Succession and Changing Property Values in Residential Chicago" (Chicago: The Committee on Education, Training, and Research in Race Relations, 1953), dittoed, as summarized in "Research Reports," Anti-Defamation League of B'Nai B'Rith, Vol. 2, No. 2, October 1955, p. 4. Also see Race Relations Department, American Missionary Association, "If Your Next Neighbors are Negroes"; Johnson, *Patterns of Negro Segregation,* pp. 201-205, for some rationalizations dealing with housing specifically.

10. See Myrdal, *op. cit.,* pp. 60-61, 66-67, 587-588.

11. For various examples of types of violence, see "If Your Next Neighbors are Negroes," p. 1; Weaver, *The Negro Ghetto,* pp. 96-97; Johnson, *Patterns of Negro Segregation,* p. 273; Edward Byron Reuter, *The American Race Problem* (rev. ed.; New York: Thomas Y. Crowell Co., 1938), pp. 404-407; Harvey Warren Zorbaugh, *The Gold Coast and the Slum* (Chicago: The University of Chicago Press, 1944), p. 148; Drake and Cayton, *op. cit.,* pp. 178-181; Myrdal, *op. cit.,* pp. 558-569. Also see K. L. Little, *Negroes in Britain* (London: Kegan Paul, Trench, Trubner and Co., 1948), pp. 57-59, for examples of what can happen in other countries.

12. For what few examples there are of this technique as well as of excuses, see J. Howell Atwood *et al., Thus Be Their Destiny* (Washington, D. C.: American Council on Education, 1941), p. 79; Charles S. Johnson, *Growing Up in the Black Belt* (Washington, D. C.: American Council on Education, 1941), pp. 287-288; Davie, *op. cit.,* p. 290; Myrdal, *op. cit.,* p. 630.

13. Myrdal, *op. cit.*

14. For illustrations of this type of pressure in housing, see Weaver, *The Negro Ghetto,* pp. 215-227; Roi Ottley, 'New World A-Coming' (New York: Literary Classics, Inc., 1943), p. 181.

15. For examples of this technique in housing, see Herman H. Long and Charles S. Johnson, *People vs. Property* (Nashville: Fisk University Press, 1947); "If Your Next Neighbors are Negroes," pp. 9-11; Weaver, *The Negro Ghetto,* pp. 211-215; Charles Abrams, *The Future of Housing* (New York: Harper and Bros., 1946), pp. 25, 90-91. For the only mention of it encountered with regard to social and religious groups, see Myrdal, *op. cit.,* pp. 638-639.

16. The over-all situation and trend here has been well outlined by Alfred McClung Lee, *Fraternities Without Brotherhood* (Boston: The Beacon Press, 1955).

17. For examples of white paternalistic attitudes encouraging segregation, principally in the South, see Johnson, *Patterns of Negro Segregation,* pp. 224-225; Myrdal, op. cit., pp. 395, 404, 459, 592-595, 769; John G. Van Deusen, *The Black Man in White America* (rev. ed.; Washington, D. C.: Associated Publishers, Inc., 1944), p. 206; Reuter, *op. cit.,* pp. 314-315.

18. See Ottley, *op. cit.,* p. 31, for the closest approximation of this technique found elsewhere in the literature.

19. For a Southerner's satirical approach to the problem of Negro-white "social" contact, see Harry Golden, "The Golden Vertical Plan," *Carolina Israelite,* as quoted in *New South,* Vol. 11, No. 11, November 1956, p. 12.

20. Examples of this type of technique are usually found only with reference to public facilities. See Myrdal, *op. cit.*, p. 631; Drake and Cayton, *op. cit.*, p. 192.

21. For a thorough discussion of these two additional factors, see Myrdal, *op. cit.*, pp. 40-42, 382-385, 600, 657-659. Also see Sumner, *op. cit.*, pp. 12-15, 29, where he discusses in-group and out-group relations which are usually at the basis of these two factors.

22. For a description of this Audit, see the *New York Times*, June 13, 1948.

23. For a more complete discussion of this Negro tendency, see Johnson, *Growing Up in the Black Belt*, pp. 82-83, 294-296; Johnson, *Patterns of Negro Segregation*, pp. 267-293.

24. For further examples of this and some of its results, see Atwood *et al.*, *op. cit.*, p. 4; Johnson, *Growing Up in the Black Belt*, pp. 299-301; Robert Austin Warner, *New Haven Negroes* (New Haven: Yale University Press, 1940), p. 184.

25. For other examples of this Negro fear, see Davie, *op. cit.*, p. 291; Myrdal, *op. cit.*, pp. 389, 602; Johnson, *Patterns of Negro Segregation*, pp. 151-152, 290-291.

26. This feeling has not been emphasized enough in American race relations literature. See Myrdal, *op. cit.*, p. 604. For a better example of how this fear operates, see Little, *op. cit.*, pp. 256-257.

27. See Franklin Henry Giddings, *The Principles of Sociology* (New York: Macmillan and Co., 1896), pp. 17-20; Sumner, *op. cit.*, pp. 12-15, 29; Reuter, *op. cit.*, pp. 386-388, 396-399; E. Franklin Frazier, *The Negro in the United States* (New York: The Macmillan Co., 1949), pp. 533-539, for additional references and examples of this kind of feeling, particularly as it applies to Negroes.

28. See Atwood *et al.*, *op. cit.*, pp. 5, 73; Myrdal, *op. cit.*, p. 619; Reuter, *op. cit.*, pp. 388-390; Johnson, *Patterns of Negro Segregation*, pp. 252-253, 277.

29. For a more thorough discussion of this phenomenon, see Drake and Cayton, *op. cit.*, pp. 390-395, 443-445; Davie, *op. cit.*, pp. 441, 444-447; Johnson, *Growing Up in the Black Belt*, pp. 242-246.

30. A good example of this sort of Negro pressure on other Negroes is seen in Johnson, *Growing Up in the Black Belt*, p. 87.

31. This Negro tendency applies, as might be expected, to the South and Southern Negroes primarily. See John Dollard, *Caste and Class in a Southern Town* (New Haven: Yale University Press, 1937), pp. 261-263; Johnson, *Patterns of Negro Segregation*, pp. 253-255.

32. See Myrdal, *op. cit.*, p. 647; Johnson, *Patterns of Negro Segregation*, pp. 275-283, 288, for other instances of Negro pride.

33. For such an important factor, practically nothing has been said about this in a systematic fashion.

34. For the potential ramifications of this factor, see E. Franklin Frazier, "Human—All Too Human," *Survey Graphic*, Vol. 36, January 1947, pp. 74-75, 99-100; Weaver, *The Negro Ghetto*, pp. 44-51; Davie. *op. cit.*, pp. 116, 121, 203.

35. This is discussed more completely elsewhere. See Dollard, *op. cit.*, pp. 250, 254-255; Johnson, *Patterns of Negro Segregation*, pp. 244-266; Davie, *op. cit.*, pp. 435-436.

36. Other aspects and examples of lack of aggressiveness are seen in

Drake and Cayton, *op. cit.*, p. 338; Johnson, *Growing Up in the Black Belt*, pp. 296-297; Johnson, *Patterns of Negro Segregation*, pp. 212-213.

37. For a more thorough discussion of Negro organization and leadership, and its operation and possibilities in various types of communities, see Cox, *op. cit.*, pp. 572-575; Myrdal, *op. cit.*, pp. 711, 722-724, 727, 733, 777-779; Davie, *op. cit.*, pp. 449-455; Ottley, *op. cit.*, pp. 236-237.

38. Contrast the position of this small-town church leadership with that of Negro churches in larger Northern and Southern cities, and in particular with such men as Rev. Martin Luther King of Montgomery, Ala.

39. It is interesting to note Eric Hoffer's comments in *The True Believer* (New York: New American Library, 1958) on the conditions under which rebellion and social change occur.

CHAPTER FIVE

Summary and Interpretations

1. See Allison Davis and John Dollard, *Children of Bondage* (Washington, D. C.: American Council on Education, 1940); John Dollard, *Caste and Class in a Southern Town* (New Haven: Yale University Press, 1937); J. Howell Atwood *et al.*, *Thus Be Their Destiny* (Washington, D. C.: American Council on Education, 1941); Allison Davis, Burleigh B. Gardner, and Mary R. Gardner, *Deep South* (Chicago: The University of Chicago Press, 1941); E. Franklin Frazier, *Negro Youth at the Crossways* (Washington, D. C.: American Council on Education, 1940); Hortense Powdermaker, *After Freedom* (New York: The Viking Press, 1939); Charles S. Johnson, *Growing Up in the Black Belt* (Washington, D. C.: American Council on Education, 1941); Bertram Wilbur Doyle, *The Etiquette of Race Relations in the South* (Chicago: The University of Chicago Press, 1937); among others.

2. See Oliver Cromwell Cox, *Caste, Class, and Race* (Garden City, New York: Doubleday and Co., 1948), pp. 354-355.

3. See W. I. Thomas, *The Unadjusted Girl* (Boston: Little, Brown, and Co., 1923), pp. 41-44, for the original theory on the definition of the situation.

4. See Louis Wirth, *The Ghetto* (Chicago: The University of Chicago Press, 1928), p. 26.

5. See Jerome K. Myers, "The Differential Time Factor in Assimilation: A Study of Aspects and Processes of Assimilation among the Italians of New Haven" (Unpublished Ph.D. dissertation, Yale University, 1950), where the same development has already been noted for New Haven Italians.

6. Thus, it is found for example even in the all-white community of Plainville. Cf. James West, *Plainville, U.S.A.* (New York: Columbia University Press, 1945), pp. 19-25.

7. An interesting manifestation of changing attitudes among Negro youth toward discrimination is seen in the recent rash of student sit-down strikes in the South.

Annotated Bibliography

Annotated Bibliography

References have been classified into four categories and are listed alphabetically within each of these. The most important sources are indicated by an asterisk.

Historical and Background Sources

ATWATER, EDWARD E. *History of The Colony of New Haven to its absorption into Connecticut.* New Haven: Printed for the Author, 1881. A thorough study of New Haven's early years with an historical background of the founding of the colony. It contains much primary source material, but it is not adequately documented and footnoted.

BALDWIN, REV. ELIJAH C. [Miscellaneous Comments on Branford], *The Home World*, Vol. 2, No. 11, 1888, pp. 641-704.

————. "Branford Annals, 1700-1800," *Papers of the New Haven Colony Historical Society*, Vol. 4, 1888, pp. 299-329.

Branford Directory 1950. New Haven: The Price and Lee Co., 1950.

The Branford Review. The current weekly newspaper.

Branford, Town of, Official Statistics:
   Births, Marriages and Deaths, Town of Branford, Vol. 1863-1895.
   Births, Marriages and Deaths, 1942-1950.
   Branford Land Records, Vols. 22, 23, 25, 30, 45, 48, 52, 71.
   Town Records, Electors since 1840.
   Town Votes, 1786-1840, Births, Marriages and Deaths, Vol. 3.

CARR, JOHN C. *Old Branford*, Branford, Conn.: The Branford Printing Co., [1935?]. A popular history in booklet form.

GILLETT, REV. TIMOTHY P. *The Past and the Present, in the Secular and Religious History of the Congregational Church and Society of Branford: A Semi-Centennial Discourse.* New Haven: Morehouse & Taylor, 1858. In *Connecticut Churches,* Vol. 1. A history of Branford woven around the history of the Congregational Church there.

*GREENE, LORENZO JOHNSTON. *The Negro in Colonial New England, 1620-1776.* New York: Columbia University Press, 1942. The most comprehensive study of slavery and Negro-white relations in Colonial New England. "A survey of New England's slave trade and the sale of Negroes in its slave markets is followed by a discussion of the social, political and economic repercussions of the buying and selling of slaves upon Puritan institutions."

KING, C. WENDELL. "Branford Center: A Community Study in Social Cleavage." Unpublished Ph.D. dissertation, Yale University, 1943. A good study of Branford dealing largely with religious and nationality groups. It contains some interesting background material.

LAMBERT, EDWARD R. *History of the Colony of New Haven before and after the Union with Connecticut, containing a particular description of the towns which composed that government, viz., New Haven, Milford, Guilford, Branford, Stamford, and Southhold, Long Island with a notice of the towns which have been set off from "The Original Six."* New Haven: Hitchcock and Stafford, 1838. A superficial study of the Colony of New Haven. Branford is mentioned almost only in passing, pp. 172-175.

*LAUBER, ALMON WHEELER. *Indian Slavery in Colonial Times within the Present Limits of the United States.* New York: Columbia University, 1913. *Studies in History, Economics and Public Law,* Vol. 54, No. 3, edited by the Faculty of Political Science of Columbia University. The best study of Indian slavery before the Revolution. See especially pp. 105-153.

Manual of the Congregational Church in Branford, Conn. New Haven: Morehouse & Taylor, 1859. In *Connecticut Churches,* Vol. 1. "A catalogue of all persons" who were members of the church from March 1688, to May 1859, with Negroes identified as such. Also includes a definition of Congregationalism, Articles of Faith, etc.

MITCHELL, MARY HEWITT. *History of New Haven County, Connecticut,* Vol. 1. Chicago: The Pioneer Historical Publishing Co., 1930. A topical treatment of the county "as a unit, rather than as the sum of a number of towns within a prescribed geographical area." It contains no footnotes or references, but seems quite authoritative.

NORTON, FREDERICK CALVIN. "Negro Slavery in Connecticut," *The Connecticut Magazine,* Vol. V, No. 6, June 1899, pp. 320-328. A good short history of the Negro in Connecticut up to 1856, but containing no footnotes.

ROCKEY, J. L. (ed.). *History of New Haven County, Connecticut,* 2 Vols. New York: W. W. Preston & Co., 1892. A fairly complete history of the county by towns up to 1890, but containing no footnotes or references. See especially Chapter I, Vol. 2, for reference to Branford.

SIMONDS, J. RUPERT. *A History of the First Church and Society of Branford, Connecticut, 1644-1919.* New Haven: The Tuttle, Morehouse & Taylor Co., [n.d.]. A history of Branford, based on the history of the Congregational Church there. It is a popularly written book with no footnotes or references.

*STEINER, BERNARD C. *History of Slavery in Connecticut.* Baltimore: The Johns Hopkins Press, 1893. *Johns Hopkins University Studies in Historical and Political Science,* Eleventh Series, IX-X. HERBERT B. ADAMS, ed. An excellent legalistic treatment of slavery in Connecticut.

U.S. Bureau of the Census:
Thirteenth Census of the United States: 1910 Population, Vol. II. Washington: Government Printing Office, 1913.
Fourteenth Census of the United States: 1920 Population, Vol. II. Washington: Government Printing Office, 1922.
Fifteenth Census of the United States: 1930 Population, Vol. III, Part 1. Washington: Government Printing Office, 1932.

Seventeenth Census of the United States: 1950 Population, Vol. 1. Washington: Government Printing Office, 1952.

*WARNER, ROBERT AUSTIN. *New Haven Negroes: A Social History*. New Haven: Yale University Press, 1940. A valuable historical and sociological study of "the manners, customs, and social position of the Negroes of New Haven."

Social Control

*BERNARD, L. L. *Social Control in its Sociological Aspects*. New York: The Macmillan Co., 1939. A general treatise and analysis of the methods used by the agents of social control. A comprehensive and competent sociological evaluation of the techniques of control.

BREARLEY, H. C. "The Nature of Social Control," *Sociology and Social Research,* Vol. 28, No. 2, November-December 1943, pp. 95-102.

*DOWD, JEROME. *Control in Human Societies*. New York: D. Appleton-Century Co., 1936. A general presentation of the evolutionary aspects of social control with emphasis on the problems of control particularly as they apply to Western Civilization.

ELIOT, THOMAS D. "Human Controls as Situation-Processes," *American Sociological Review,* Vol. 8, No. 4, August 1943, pp. 380-388. "An argument for the adoption of a terminology of social interaction and controls better adopted to the now accepted viewpoints of physics, biology, and general semantics."

EVERETT, HELEN. "Control, Social," *Encyclopaedia of the Social Sciences,* EDWIN R. A. SELIGMAN, ed., Vol. 4, pp. 344-348. New York: The Macmillan Co., 1937. Largely economic in orientation.

*HOLLINGSHEAD, A. B. "The Concept of Social Control," *American Sociological Review,* Vol. 6, No. 2, April 1941, pp. 217-224. A re-examination of the concept of social control from the point of view of social organization in the attempt to develop "a theoretical foundation from which to derive tentative propositions of an abstract nature (hypotheses) capable of empirical test."

HOLLINGWORTH, LETA S. "Social Devices for Impelling Women to Bear and Rear Children," *American Journal of Sociology,* Vol. 22, No. 1, July 1916, pp. 19-29.

KALLEN, HORACE M. "Conformity," *Encyclopaedia of the Social Sciences,* EDWIN R. A. SELIGMAN, ed., Vol. 4, pp. 196-198. New York: The Macmillan Co., 1937.

*LANDIS, PAUL H. *Social Control: Social Organization and Disorganization in Process.* Chicago: J. B. Lippincott Co., 1956, rev. ed. A detailed approach to social control emphasizing "the deterministic influence of social and cultural environments in shaping personality."

*LAPIERE, RICHARD T. *A Theory of Social Control.* New York: McGraw-Hill Book Co., 1954. Probably the best and most up-to-date text on this subject yet published.

LEMERT, EDWIN M. "Legal Commitment and Social Control," *Sociology and Social Research,* Vol. 30, No. 4, May-June 1946, pp. 370-378.

—————. "The Folkways and Social Control," *American Sociological Review,* Vol. 7, No. 3, June 1942, pp. 394-399.

*—————. "The Grand Jury as an Agency of Social Control," *American Sociological Review,* Vol. 10, No. 6, December 1945, pp. 751-758. The advancement of a "hypothetical system for the analysis of social control situations."

*LUMLEY, FREDERICK ELMORE. *Means of Social Control.* New York: The Century Co., 1925. A detailed description of many means of enforcing norms of conduct. Lumley lists fourteen topics: rewards, praise, flattery, persuasion, advertising, slogans, propaganda, gossip, satire, laughter, calling names, commands, threats, and punishment.

MEAD, MARGARET. "Tabu," *Encyclopaedia of the Social Sciences,* EDWIN R. A. SELIGMAN, ed., Vol. 14, pp. 502-505. New York: The Macmillan Co., 1937. Discussed from an anthropological point of view.

RADCLIFFE-BROWN, A. R. "Sanctions, Social," *Encyclopaedia of the Social Sciences,* EDWIN R. A. SELIGMAN, ed., Vol. 13, pp. 531-534. New York: The Macmillan Co., 1937.

*ROSS, EDWARD ALSWORTH. *Social Control: A Survey of the Foundations of Order.* New York: The Macmillan Co., 1901. A pioneer volume with a description of the means, nature, and processes of social control. While reflecting

certain psychological positions now outdated, it still remains the most complete systematic exposition of the
field of social control. Discusses public opinion, law,
belief, social suggestion, education, custom, religion,
personal ideals, ceremony, art, personality, enlighten-
ment, illusion, and social valuations.

*ROUCEK, JOSEPH S., and associates. *Social Control.* New
York: D. Van Nostrand Co., Inc., 1947. A symposium
devoted to a study of the field of social control. It
emphasizes not only the means and techniques of control but also the part played by institutions.

*SEGERSTEDT, TORGNY T. "Social Control as Sociological Con-
cept," *Uppsala Universitets Arsskrift,* Vol. 5, 1948. A
provocative attempt "to explain social uniformity by
social causes, even if science cannot always carry causal
explanation beyond the fixing of certain correlations."

Race Relations

*ABRAMS, CHARLES. *Forbidden Neighbors: A Study of Prej-
udice in Housing.* New York: Harper & Bros., 1955. One
of the best written and most valuable books to appear on
this subject in recent years.

————. *The Future of Housing.* New York: Harper and
Bros., 1946.

*ATWOOD, J. HOWELL, DONALD W. WYATT, VINCENT J. DAVIS,
and IRA D. WALKER. *Thus Be Their Destiny: The Personality Development of Negro Youth in Three Communities.* Washington, D.C.: American Council on Education, 1941. How Negro boys and girls grow up in three
small cities of liberal tradition, two Northern and one
Southern.

BANKS, W. S. M., II. "The Rank Order of Sensitivity to Discriminations of Negroes in Columbus, Ohio," *American
Sociological Review,* Vol. 15, No. 4, August 1950, pp.
529-534.

*BLALOCK, H. M. "Economic Discrimination and Negro In-
crease," *American Sociological Review,* Vol. 21, No. 5,
October 1956, pp. 584-588. One of the more provocative
and fruitful articles of recent years which have analyzed
the relationship between these two factors. Suggests that

the traditional generalization needs badly to be qualified or clarified.

BOURNE, HENRY T., JR. "Young and Colored: A Study of the Educational Ideals and Problems of Negro School Children in New Haven." Unpublished Senior Essay, Yale Sociology Department, 1949.

BOYKIN, ULYSSES W. *A Hand Book on the Detroit Negro*. Detroit: The Minority Study Associates, 1943. A brief historical study of Negro "adjustments and readjustments."

BRAND, MILLEN. *Albert Sears*. New York: Simon and Schuster, 1947. A story of a colored family which moves into a block occupied by white persons.

BROWN, FRANCIS J. and JOSEPH SLABEY ROUCEK (eds.). *One America: The History, Contributions, and Present Problems of Our Racial and National Minorities*. New York: Prentice-Hall, Inc., 1945, rev. ed. A compendium of information about our foreign populations. See especially pp. 29-32, 450-461, 588-615.

BROWN, G. GORDON. *Legal Administration and Negro-White Relations in Philadelphia: A Study in Race Relations*. Philadelphia: Bureau of Municipal Research of Philadelphia, 1947. A study of the position of the Negro in Philadelphia and of his relation to the police and other law enforcement agencies in particular.

CAYTON, HORACE R. and GEORGE S. MITCHELL. *Black Workers and the New Unions*. Chapel Hill: The University of North Carolina Press, 1939. A study of Negro workers in three industries: iron and steel, meat-packing, and railroad car shops.

CHATTO, CLARENCE I. and ALICE L. HALLIGAN. *The Story of the Springfield Plan: One Community's Total War Against Prejudice*. New York: Barnes and Noble, Inc., 1945. The official description of how the schools are leading the community in Springfield's campaign against group hatred.

CLARK, KENNETH B. and MAMIE P. CLARK. "Racial Identification and Preference in Negro Children," *Readings in Social Psychology*, THEODORE M. NEWCOMB and EUGENE L. HARTLEY, eds., pp. 169-178. New York: Henry Holt and Co., 1947.

CONNECTICUT INTER-RACIAL COMMISSION. *Connecticut Inter-Racial Survey,* Vols. II, III, and IV, May-June 1946 to Winter 1948-49.

COX, OLIVER CROMWELL. *Caste, Class and Race: A Study in Social Dynamics.* Garden City, New York: Doubleday and Co., Inc., 1948. A discussion of three social concepts in regard to their theoretical meaning and political implications in modern society. A major part of the book is concerned with the problem of racial antagonism in its relation to the political and economic class struggle within our social system and attempts to present a theory of race relations directly opposed to the caste-class hypothesis.

*DAVIE, MAURICE R. *Negroes in American Society.* New York: McGraw-Hill Book Co., 1949. A comprehensive and readable treatise on the status and role of the American Negro in the United States and of Negro-white relations from the time of his arrival through slavery to his present position in American society. Analysis is made of the development that has occurred in economic, religious, familial, political, educational, and other social and institutional aspects of Negro life.

*DAVIS, ALLISON. "The Motivation of the Underprivileged Worker," *Industry and Society,* ed. by WILLIAM FOOTE WHYTE, pp. 84-106. New York: McGraw-Hill Book Co., Inc., 1946.

*————, BURLEIGH B. GARDNER and MARY R. GARDNER. *Deep South: A Social Anthropological Study of Caste and Class.* Chicago: The University of Chicago Press, 1941. An excellent study of Negro-white relationships in a Southern community.

*————, and JOHN DOLLARD. *Children of Bondage: The Personality Development of Negro Youth in the Urban South.* Washington, D.C.: American Council on Education, 1940. An examination of "the life experiences of eight selected Negro adolescents" aimed at "revealing what it means to be born a Negro."

DAVIS, JOHN A. "Negro Employment: A Progress Report," *Fortune,* July 1952, pp. 102-103, 158, 161-162.

*DOLLARD, JOHN. *Caste and Class in a Southern Town.* New Haven: Yale University Press, 1937. Negro-white relationships as observed by a Northern psychologist in a five months' stay in a small Mississippi cotton town. A sociological study emphasizing the "gains" to whites from the caste system as well as the social, emotional, and economic problems of Negroes which arise out of the caste-class structure of the Southern town.

*DOYLE, BERTRAM WILBUR. *The Etiquette of Race Relations in the South: A Study in Social Control.* Chicago: The University of Chicago Press, 1937. Manners and customs in race relations in the South since Colonial days.

*DRAKE, ST. CLAIR and HORACE R. CAYTON. *Black Metropolis: A Study of Negro Life in a Northern City.* New York: Harcourt, Brace and Company, 1945. A comprehensive and critical analysis of the organization and structure of the Negro community in Chicago, both internally and in relation to the metropolis of which it is a part. An excellent and authoritative study of race relations in this country, it is a description of the processes and problems in the adjustment of the Negro in one city of the American urban-industrial scene, which has its counterpart in many Northern cities with large Negro populations.

EDMUNDS, EDWIN R. "The Myrdalian Thesis: Rank Order of Discrimination," *Phylon,* Vol. 15, No. 3, September 1954, pp. 297-303.

EMBREE, EDWIN R. *Brown Americans: The Story of a Tenth of the Nation.* New York: The Viking Press, 1944. An excellent presentation of the origin, development, achievements, and problems of the Negro in America, written by the president of the former Julius Rosenwald Fund.

FRAZIER, E. FRANKLIN. "Human—All Too Human," *Survey Graphic,* Vol. 36, January 1947, pp. 74-75, 99-100. An article on Negro vested interests.

*————. *Negro Youth at the Crossways: The Personality Development in the Middle States.* Washington, D.C.: American Council on Education, 1940. An analysis of interracial experiences of 268 Negro young people in Washington, D.C., and Louisville, Kentucky.

*————. *The Negro in the United States.* New York: The Macmillan Co., 1957, rev. ed. A richly documented and

comprehensive study of the "adjustment of the Negro as a racial and cultural group to the life of the larger society and the responses that society has made of his presence." The data is presented in a complete survey of the Negro in America, from his African heritage and his slavery to his current hopes of civil rights legislation.

GOLDEN, HARRY. "The Golden Vertical Plan," *Carolina Israelite,* as quoted in *New South,* Vol. 11, No. 11, November 1956, p. 12. One of the most successful and imaginative attempts at satirizing the Southern pattern of segregation. For other examples of his humor see other issues of the *Carolina Israelite.*

GOSNELL, HAROLD F. *Negro Politicians: The Rise of Negro Politics in Chicago.* Chicago: The University of Chicago Press, 1935. The views of whites about Negroes in civic affairs are also included.

*HARDIN, CLARA A. *The Negroes of Philadelphia: The Cultural Adjustment of a Minority Group.* Published Ph.D. dissertation, Byrn Mawr College, 1945. A cultural anthropological study of Negroes in Philadelphia since colonial times.

HIMES, CHESTER B. *If He Hollers Let Him Go.* Garden City, New York: Doubleday, Doran and Co., Inc., 1945. A story of racial conflict tensions inherent in a West Coast shipyard and their effect on Bob Jones, a young Negro from the Middle West.

HOROWITZ, EUGENE L. "Development of Attitude toward Negroes," *Readings in Social Psychology,* THEODORE M. NEWCOMB and EUGENE L. HARTLEY, eds., pp. 507-517. New York: Henry Holt and Co., 1947

HUGHES, LANGSTON. *Simple Speaks His Mind.* New York: Simon and Schuster, 1950.

*JOHNSON, CHARLES S. *Growing Up In the Black Belt: Negro Youth in the Rural South.* Washington, D.C.: American Council on Education, 1941. A record of "the effects upon the personality development of rural Negro youth of their membership in a minority racial group."

————, and associates. *Into the Main Stream: A Survey of Best Practices in Race Relations in the South.* Chapel Hill: The University of North Carolina Press, 1947. A study which depicts actual racial cooperation taking place between Negroes and whites in the South today in the fields of politics, employment, education, housing, health, and religion. It is also an outline of the social and economic progress of Negroes during the last quarter of a century.

*————. *Patterns of Negro Segregation*. New York: Harper and Bros., 1943. A competent and comprehensive survey of regional variations of segregation. This book arrays a large body of evidence as to the extent and character of discrimination against the Negro in America. Every phase of life into which discrimination might enter has been dispassionately examined, including politics, education, industry, recreation, social life and the rest.

————. *The Negro in American Civilization: A Study of Negro Life and Race Relations in the Light of Social Research*. New York: Henry Holt and Co,. 1930.

*————, and associates. *To Stem This Tide: A Survey of Racial Tension Areas in the United States*. Boston: The Pilgrim Press, 1943. A survey of the country at large with respect to racial tension in industry, in rural districts, on public carriers, in housing, in politics, and in the armed services. Attention is given to the sources and kinds of friction peculiar to the various sections of the country.

JOHNSON, JAMES WELDON. *Black Manhattan*. New York: Alfred A. Knopf, 1930. Negro life in New York City from Colonial times to the present day.

KATONA, ARTHUR. "A Survey of Discrimination in a Northern Town," *Social Forces,* Vol. 26, No. 4, May 1948, pp. 443-450.

KENNEDY, LOUISE VENABLE. *The Negro Peasant Turns Cityward: Effects of Recent Migrations to Northern Centers*. New York: Columbia University Press, 1930.

KLINEBERG, OTTO (ed.). *Characteristics of the American Negro*. New York: Harper and Bros., 1944. An excellent survey of what is known about Negro intelligence and personality, race attitudes, miscegenation and intermarriage, and mental diseases among American Negroes.

LA FARGE, JOHN. *The Race Question and the Negro: A Study of the Catholic Doctrine on Interracial Justice*. New York: Longmans, Green and Co., 1943.

LEE, ALFRED MCCLUNG. *Fraternities Without Brotherhood.* Boston: The Beacon Press 1955. A survey of discriminatory practices in college fraternities.

LITTLE, K. L. *Negroes in Britain: A Study of Racial Relations in English Society.* London: Kegan Paul, Trench, Trubner and Co., Ltd., 1948. An historical and cultural study of the social effects of a mixture of colored peoples in the urban population of Great Britain.

LOCKE, ALAIN, and BERNARD J. STERN (eds.). *When Peoples Meet: A Study in Race and Culture Contacts.* New York: Progressive Education Association, 1942. An anthology of specialized and authoritative writings in all branches of the social sciences on the contacts of peoples and cultures.

*LOESCHER, FRANK S. *The Protestant Church and the Negro: A Pattern of Segregation.* New York: Association Press, 1948. A survey of relations between Negro and white members of Protestant denominations in the North and the South.

LOGAN, RAYFORD W. (ed.). *What the Negro Wants.* Chapel Hill: The University of North Carolina Press, 1944. A symposium comprising the contributions of fourteen prominent Negroes who tell unevenly but effectively, on the whole, what the Negro wants as an American citizen.

*LONG, HERMAN H. and CHARLES JOHNSON. *People vs. Property: Race Restrictive Covenants in Housing.* Nashville, Tenn.: Fisk University Press, 1947. A practical analysis of restrictive covenants by so-called neighborhood improvement associations and real estate organizations in relation to the over-all question of racial segregation.

MACIVER, ROBERT MORRISON. *The More Perfect Union: A Program for the Control of Inter-Group Discrimination in the United States.* New York: The Macmillan Co., 1948.

*MCCORMICK, THOMAS C. and RICHARD A. HORNSETH. "The Negro in Madison, Wisconsin," *American Sociological Review,* Vol. 12, No. 5, October 1947, pp. 519-525. One of the few studies available on the Negro in a Northern city. It discusses the high rates of stability and transiency of the Negro population in relation to the meager economic opportunities available to them.

McWilliams, Carey. *Brothers Under the Skin.* Boston: Little, Brown and Co., 1943. The color problem in America, with a practical program for dealing with race problems and minority groups.

Manning, Seaton Wesley. "Negro Trade Unionists in Boston," *Social Forces,* Vol. 17, No. 2, December 1938, pp. 256-266.

Minnesota, The State of. *Race Relations in Minnesota.* Reports of the Governor's Interracial Commission. Saint Paul, Minn.: The Commission, 1948. A survey covering employment and housing conditions for Negroes as well as the status of Indians and Mexicans.

Moon, Bucklin. *The Darker Brother.* Garden City, New York: Doubleday, Doran and Co., Inc., 1943. The story of a young Southern Negro boy and his widowed mother who came north from Florida to live in Harlem.

————. *The High Cost of Prejudice.* New York: Julian Messner, Inc., 1947. An excellent analysis of the cost and effects of discrimination and prejudices against both the Negroes and whites in America, examined in such areas as industry, politics, education, and the armed services.

*Moon, Henry Lee. *Balance of Power*: *The Negro Vote.* Garden City, New York: Doubleday and Co., Inc., 1948.

Moton, Robert Russa. *What the Negro Thinks.* Garden City, New York: Doubleday, Doran and Co., 1929. Thoughts of the Negro on racial discrimination and the experiences he is subjected to because of his color. The author believes Negroes are more likely to know whites than vice versa.

Murray, Florence (ed.). *The Negro Handbook, 1949.* New York: The Macmillan Co., 1949. "A manual of current facts and statistics concerning Negroes in the United States." A biennial reference book.

*Myrdal, Gunnar. *An American Dilemma*: *The Negro Problem and Modern Democracy.* New York: Harper and Bros., 1944. The most comprehensive and scholarly study of the Negro in American society. It analyzes anthropological, cultural, social, economic, legal, political, educational, and spiritual aspects of the Negro minority, set against the background of the American

Creed. The dilemma between American ideals and social concepts and the actual behavior of white towards Negro and vice versa represents a "moral lag in the development of the nation."

*NATIONAL URBAN LEAGUE, DEPARTMENT OF RESEARCH. *A Review of the Social and Economic Conditions of the Negro Population of Hartford, Connecticut.* New York: September-October 1944.

—————. *Social Condtions of the Negro in The Hill District of Pittsburgh.* IRA DEA. REID, Director. Pittsburgh: Published by the General Committee on the Hill Survey, 1930.

NORTHRUP, HERBERT R. "Discrimination and the Trade Unions," *Discrimination and National Welfare,* ed. by R. M. MACIVER, New York: Institute for Religious and Social Studies, 1949, pp. 65-76.

*—————. *Organized Labor and the Negro.* New York: Harper and Bros., 1944. A carefully documented study of the racial policies of the trade unions and the status of Negroes in industry since the last depression. It shows how exclusion exists through ritual, constitutional provisions, tacit consent, and segregated auxiliary status and how such external factors as regional differences, the labor supply, and the presence of Negroes in industries being unionized by the C.I.O. also have influenced policy.

*OTTLEY, ROI. *'New World A-Coming.'* New York: Literary Classics, Inc., 1943. A distinguished Negro journalist's account of what American Negroes are doing and thinking and of how they are living presented against the background of Harlem in New York City. He traces the history of Harlem from its earliest days to World War II.

PARK, ROBERT E. *Race and Culture.* Glencoe, Illinois: The Free Press, 1950. The collected papers on race relations of a sociologist who trained a generation of sociologists, comprising "the record of a passionate but speculative man's thinking about a great theme of human life and history."

PORCH, MARVIN E. *The Philadelphia Main Line Negro: A Social, Economic, and Educational Survey.* Published

Ph.D. dissertation, Teachers' College of Temple University, 1938.

*POWDERMAKER, HORTENSE. *After Freedom: A Cultural Study in the Deep South.* New York: The Viking Press, 1939. An anthropologist's study of a Southern community in Mississippi.

PRESIDENT'S COMMITTEE ON CIVIL RIGHTS. *To Secure These Rights.* New York: Simon and Schuster, 1947. A study of the chief types of civil rights violations in all sections of the United States, together with recommendations for government action to achieve these rights for all groups.

RACE RELATIONS DEPARTMENT, AMERICAN MISSIONARY ASSOCIATION. "If Your Next Neighbors are Negroes." n. d.

*REID, IRA DEA. *In A Minor Key: Negro Youth in Story and Fact.* Washington, D.C.: American Council on Education, 1940. A collection of facts and figures on the conditions facing American Negro youth.

REUTER, EDWARD BYRON. *The American Race Problem: A Study of the Negro.* New York: Thomas Y. Crowell Co., 1938, rev. ed. A comprehensive and historical treatment of the race problem.

RICHMOND, ANTHONY H. "Economic Insecurity and Stereotypes as Factors in Color Prejudice," *The Sociological Review,* Vol. XLII, Section 8, 1950.

ROSE, ARNOLD and CAROLINE. *America Divided: Minority Group Relations in the United States.* New York: Alfred A. Knopf, 1948. A survey of racial, religious, and ethnic antagonisms in terms of social consequences to both majority and minority groups, to international relations, and to future history. It is also a survey and summary of the history, present status, problems, and future outlook of the principal minority groups in the United States.

ROSE, ARNOLD MARSHALL. *The Negro's Morale: Group Identification and Protest.* Minneapolis: University of Minnesota Press, 1949. An analysis of the Negro's group feeling, examining both the history of the American Negro and contemporary Negro life in terms of the individual's sense of belonging both to the subgroup of American Negroes and to the total American community.

*————. *The Negro in America.* New York: Harper and

Bros., 1948. A frank condensation of Gunnar Myrdal's *An American Dilemma.*

*Ross, MALCOLM. *All Manner of Men.* New York: Reynal and Hitchcock, 1948. A study largely devoted to the government's wartime experiment with the Fair Employment Practice Committee as seen from Mr. Ross's experience as chairman of that agency.

SCHIETINGER, E. F. "Racial Succession and Changing Property Values in Residential Chicago," Chicago: The Committee on Education, Training and Research in Race Relations, 1953, dittoed, as summarized in *Research Reports,* Anti-Defamation League of B'Nai B'Rith, Vol. 2, No. 2, October 1955, p. 4.

*SIMPSON, GEORGE EATON and J. MILTON YINGER. *Racial and Cultural Minorities.* New York: Harper and Bros., 1953, rev. ed. The best text on both the nature of prejudice and America's various minority groups. It is approached from an institutional point of view.

SOUTHERN REGIONAL COUNCIL. "Changing Patterns in the New South," Vols. 9 and 10, December-January 1954-1955.

SPRAGUE, THEODORE W., "The Rivalry of Intolerances in Race Relations," *Social Forces,* Vol. 28, No. 1, October 1949, pp. 68-76.

STERNER, RICHARD, and associates. *The Negro's Share: A Study of Income, Consumption, Housing and Public Assistance.* New York: Harper and Bros., 1943.

SUTHERLAND, ROBERT L. *Color, Class, and Personality.* Washington, D.C.: American Council on Education, 1942. A summary of the findings of the various studies of the American Youth Commission on Negro youth, together with an interpretation of how they may be used for improving their status.

*TANNENBAUM, FRANK. *Slave and Citizen: The Negro in the Americas.* New York: Alfred A. Knopf, 1947. An historical study of the race problem in the United States and Latin America, valuable for cross-cultural comparison of the evolution of the status of Negroes. The writer demonstrates that the national history and religious background of the European home communities strongly affected attitudes toward slavery.

THOMPSON, EDGAR T. (ed.). *Race Relations and the Race Problem: A Definition and An Analysis.* Durham, N.C.: Duke University Press, 1939.

VAN DEUSEN, JOHN G. *The Black Man in White America.* Washington, D.C.: Associated Publishers, Inc., 1944, rev. ed.

WALKER, HARRY J. "Changes in Race Accommodation in a Southern Community." Unpublished Ph.D. dissertation, University of Chicago, 1945.

WEATHERFORD, WILLIS D. and CHARLES S. JOHNSON. *Race Relations: Adjustment of Whites and Negroes in the United States.* Boston: D. C. Heath and Co., 1934. An historical treatment.

WEAVER, ROBERT C. "Effect on Housing," *Discrimination and National Welfare,* ed. by R. M. MACIVER, pp. 25-35. New York: Institute for Religious and Social Studies, 1949.

*————. *Negro Labor: A National Problem.* New York: Harcourt, Brace and Co., 1946. An analysis and interpretation of Negro labor in the United States during the war years, together with a discussion of implications for the future.

*————. *The Negro Ghetto.* New York: Harcourt, Brace and Co., 1948. A clear account of the rise, development, and results of enforced residential segregation in Northern sections of the country.

WHITE, W. L. *Lost Boundaries.* New York: Harcourt, Brace and Co., 1948. A true story of a Negro family which passed for white for many years in a New England town, and the social and psychological consequences to it of the revelation of "Negro blood."

WILLIAMS, ROBIN M., JR. *The Reduction of Intergroup Tensions: A Survey of Research on Problems of Ethnic, Racial, and Religious Group Relations.* New York: Social Science Research Council, Bulletin 57, 1947.

WOOFTER, T. J., JR. *Negro Problems in Cities.* Garden City, New York: Doubleday, Doran and Co., Inc., 1928. A study of Negro neighborhoods, housing, schools, and recreation in seven Northern and nine Southern cities.

WORK PROJECTS ADMINISTRATION. *The Negroes of Nebraska.* Lincoln, Nebraska: Woodruff Printing Co., 1940. A brief historical study.

WRIGHT, RICHARD. *Black Boy*: *A Record of Childhood and Youth*. New York: Harper and Bros., 1945. An autobiography of years lived in the South wherein the repressive influences of the social environment are vividly portrayed.

————. *Native Son*. New York: Harper and Bros., 1940. The crippling effects of frustration and fear on a Negro youth in American society.

General Literature

*COOLEY, CHARLES HORTON. *Human Nature and the Social Order*. New York: C. Scribner's Sons, 1902. An early social psychological study.

*DAVIS, KINGSLEY. *Human Society*. New York: The Macmillan Co., 1949.

DAWSON, CARL A. and WARNER E. GETTYS. *An Introduction to Sociology*. New York: The Ronald Press Co., 1929. See especially Chapter 17 for social control.

ELLSWORTH, JOHN S., JR. *Factory Folkways*: *A Study of Institutional Structure and Change*. New Haven: Yale University Press, 1952. A study of a factory in a small New England town. It refers to the New England hostility toward non-local personages, particularly when they are readily identifiable, i.e., Negroes.

ELLWOOD, CHARLES A. *An Introduction to Social Psychology*, New York: D. Appleton and Co., 1917. One of the early works dealing with social control.

EUBANK, EARLE EDWARD. *The Concepts of Sociology*: *A Treatise Presenting a Suggested Organization of Sociological Theory in Terms of its Major Concepts*. Boston: D. C. Heath and Co., 1932. See especially Chapter 11 for social control.

FARIS, ELLSWORTH. *The Nature of Human Nature*: *And Other Essays in Social Psychology*. New York: McGraw-Hill Book Co., Inc., 1937.

FIRTH, RAYMOND. *Elements of Social Organization*. New York: Philosophical Library, 1951.

*GIDDINGS, FRANKLIN HENRY. *The Principles of Sociology*: *An Analysis of the Phenomena of Association and of Social*

Organization. New York: Macmillan and Co., 1896. An early psychological study where he developed his theory of consciousness of kind.

*GILLIN, JOHN LEWIS and JOHN PHILIP GILLIN. *Cultural Sociology*. New York: The Macmillan Co., 1948, rev. ed. A good presentation of the cultural point of view. See also Chapter 28 on social control.

HANKINS, FRANK HAMILTON. *An Introduction to the Study of Society: An Outline of Primary Factors and Fundamental Institutions*. New York: The Macmillan Co., 1930. See especially pp. 359-374 for social control.

*HERTZLER, J. O. *Social Institutions*. Lincoln, Nebraska: University of Nebraska Press, 1946. A good institutional approach. See especially pp. 10-13, 325-326 for social control.

HOFFER, ERIC. *The True Believer*. New York: New American Library, 1958.

*HOMANS, GEORGE C. *The Human Group*. New York: Harcourt, Brace and Co., 1950.

*KELLER, ALBERT GALLOWAY. *Societal Evolution: A Study of the Evolutionary Basis of the Science of Society*. New York: The Macmillan Co., 1931, rev. ed. A classic cultural presentation. Stresses the importance of the economic mores.

LANDIS, PAUL H. *Man in Environment: An Introduction to Sociology*. New York: Thomas Y. Crowell Co., 1949. See especially Chapters 24, 25, and 32 for social control.

LEE, ALFRED McCLUNG (ed.). *New Outline of the Principles of Sociology*. New York: Barnes and Noble, Inc., 1946. See especially pp. 131-164 by Edward B. Reuter on race and culture and pp. 267-281 by Everett Cherrington Hughes on social control.

LUMLEY, FREDERICK E. *Principles of Sociology*. New York: McGraw-Hill Book Co., Inc., 1928. A cultural study. See especially Chapter 23 for social control.

*MALINOWSKI, BRONISLAW. *The Dynamics of Culture Change: An Inquiry into Race Relations in Africa*. New Haven: Yale University Press, 1945. The author's views on the the problem of race where the white man has moved into territories occupied by men of a different color.

*MYERS, JEROME K. "The Differential Time Factor in Assimilation: A Study of Aspects and Processes of Assimilation among the Italians of New Haven." Unpublished Ph.D. dissertation, Yale University, 1950.

NEWCOMB, THEODORE M. and EUGENE L. HARTLEY (eds.). *Readings in Social Psychology.* New York: Henry Holt and Co., 1947. A good symposium with many valuable articles.

*OGBURN, WILLIAM F. and MEYER F. NIMKOFF. *Sociology.* Boston: Houghton Mifflin Co., 1940. An excellent introductory text stressing the effects of "heredity, geographical environment, the group, and culture."

*PANUNZIO, CONSTANTINE. *Major Social Institutions: An Introduction.* New York: The Macmillan Co., 1939. A good presentation of the institutional approach. See especially Chapter 28 for social control.

PARK, ROBERT E. and ERNEST W. BURGESS. *Introduction to the Science of Sociology.* Chicago: The University of Chicago Press, 1921.

RAPPORT, VICTOR A. "Conflict in a New England College Town," *Social Forces.* Vol. 17, No. 4, May 1939, pp. 527-532.

REUTER, EDWARD BYRON. *Handbook of Sociology.* New York: The Dryden Press, 1941. A "dictionary" for the student. See especially pp. 102-103 for social control.

*REUTER, E. B. and C. W. HART. *Introduction to Sociology.* New York: McGraw-Hill Book Co., 1933. See especially Chapter 15 for social control.

ROSS, EDWARD ALSWORTH. *New-Age Sociology.* New York: D. Appleton-Century Co., Inc., 1940. See especially Chapter 34 for social control.

ROUCEK, JOSEPH S. and ROLAND L. WARREN. *Sociology: An Introduction.* Ames, Iowa: Littlefield, Adams and Co., 1951. See especially Chapter 19 for social control.

*SLOTKIN, J. S. *Social Anthropology: The Science of Human Society and Culture.* New York: The Macmillan Co., 1950. See especially Chapters 15 and 16 for social control.

SMALL, ALBION W. and GEORGE E. VINCENT. *An Introduction to the Study of Society.* New York: American Book Co., 1894.

*SUMNER, WILLIAM GRAHAM. *Folkways: A Study of the Sociological Importance of Usages, Manners, Customs, Mores,* *and Morals.* Boston: Ginn & Co., 1906. See especially Chapters 1, 2, and 15. Also has analysis of in-group and out-group concept.

THOMAS, WILLIAM I. *The Unadjusted Girl: with cases and standpoint for behavior analysis.* Boston: Little, Brown, and Co., 1923. Criminal Science Monograph No. 4.

WEST, JAMES. *Plainville, U.S.A.* New York: Columbia University Press, 1945.

WIRTH, LOUIS. *The Ghetto.* Chicago: The University of Chicago Press, 1928. A sociological analysis of Jewish life in Europe and America, and containing some similarities to Negro life in the United States.

*YOUNG, KIMBALL. *Social Psychology.* New York: F. S. Crofts and Co., Inc., 1945, second ed. See especially Chapter 22 for social control.

*————. *Sociology: A Study of Society and Culture.* New York: American Book Co., 1942. See especially Chapter 33 for social control.

ZORBAUGH, HARVEY WARREN. *The Gold Coast and the Slum: A Sociological Study of Chicago's Near North Side.* Chicago: The University of Chicago Press, 1944.

Index

Index

Absenteeism, affects Negro job advancement, 47, 82

Aggressiveness, Negro lack of, results in acceptance of race relations status quo, 121-22, 124

American Dilemma (Myrdal), 92

American Legion, 56, 62; Negro participation discouraged, 36, 63-64, 105

Amusements, discrimination in, 73-74; *see also* Movie theater

Antidiscrimination legislation, 31, 97; indirect evidence of discrimination, 125-26; *see also* Fair Employment Practice Act

Avoidance, Negro behavior pattern, 110-11, 122, 124, 130

Banks, deny mortages to Negroes, 28-29, 45, 72, 96; never hire Negroes, 52; service to Negroes, 72-73

Banks, W. S. M., II, 74-75

Baptist Church, Negro participation in, 33-34, 98, 105

Baptists, 16, 34

Barber and beauty shops, 27-28, 37; don't serve Negroes, 68-69, 95, 129; Negroes use own, 117, 120

Bars and taverns, 52, 116; discrimination in, 37, 69-70; techniques of refusing service to Negroes, 94-95, 105, 108-9, 129

Bathing beaches, discrimination at, 37, 70-71; why Negroes avoid, 116-17

Behavior, areas of, correspond to community interests, 18-19

Booker T. Washington Club, all-Negro athletic group, 62

Boy Scouts, 59; Negroes formerly had own units, 35-36; not regarded as segregated by Negroes, 61, 62

Catholics, *see* Roman Catholics

Chamber of Commerce, Negroes in, 63, 98

Charitable organizations, *see* Red Cross, Visiting Nurse Assn.

Churches, 57, 90, 100, 128; historically segregated, 24, 25, 27; Negroes desire own, 34-35, 117-18, 120; social activities in, 57-59, 75, 107; *see also* individual denominations

Cicero, Illinois, violence in, 92, 124

Congregational Church, Negro participation in, 27, 33, 35, 57, 59, 61; majority vote required for admission to, 98

Congregationalists, 15, 16

Congress of Industrial Organizations (CIO), 31, 75-76, 113; *see also* Unions

Connecticut Civil Rights Commission, acts against discrimination in overnight accommodations, 71-72

Connecticut Town, description of, 15-18; ethnic and religious composition of, 15-16; industry, 17; subdivisions, 17-18; background of race relations in, *1637-1900*, 23-26, *1900-1914*, 26-28, *1914-1950*, 28-38

Consciousness of kind, Negro feeling reinforcing segregation pattern, 114-18, self-awareness, 129-30

Council of Churches, Negro participation in, 57-58, 75

Courts, Negroes receive equal treatment in, 66

Cox, O. C., "Stranger Situation," 127

Crime, 37; Negro rate low, 66

Cultural development of Negro, low by white standards, 28, 37, 79, 80; rural Southern background, 32, 79; effect of, on Negro behavior, 117, 126, 127; *see also* Socioeconomic status

"Customer reaction," white reason for discriminatory job practices, 52, 88-89, 103-4, 128
"Cutting dead," white technique of social control, 48, 107-8

Daughters of the American Revolution (DAR), 56
Democratic Club, attitude toward Negroes, 68
Democratic Town Committee, no Negro members, 68
Democrats, accused by Republicans of playing politics with housing project, 43; majority of Negroes are, 37, 67-68
De Molay, Masonic youth organization, 63
Dentists, behavior toward Negroes, 52, 73
Dependability or responsibility, Negro lack of, 47, 53, 79, 82-83, 123
Direct refusal and insult, white techniques of social control, 92-95, 129
Disabled American Veterans, 63-64
Discrimination, 74-77, 79, 91, 112, 128; before 1950, 26-38; size of Negro population and, 26, 28, 38, 84-85, 123, 127; Negro resistance to, 133-34; see also Housing, Jobs, Public facilities, Schools, Social and religious activities
Doctors, behavior toward Negroes, 52, 105; Negro accounts of discrimination by, exaggerated, 73, 109; Negroes refused credit by, 82-83
Drinking, little done by Negroes, 66

Economic pressure, white technique of social control, 95-96, 119, 128; elimination of prospective Negro house buyers, 100-1; see also Institutional devices
Edmunds, E. R., 75
Education, 18, 25, 74; effect of low Negro level of, 47, 78, 79-81, 123; effect of rising Negro level of, 132, 133; see also Schools
Embarrassment and humiliation, Negro fear of, 130

Employment, effect on Negroes of low level of, 37; of high level of, 132-33; see also Jobs
Episcopal Church, 98
Episcopalians, 15, 16
Equality, spoken value of whites, 12
Ethnocentrism, see Consciousness of kind
Evasion or ignoring, white technique of social control, 105-9
Excuses, common white technique of social control in all areas of behavior, 101-5; see also Rationalizations

Fair Employment Practice Act (F.E.P.A.), Conn., 31n; ineffective, 53, 74, 76, 119, 132, 133
Fighting and stoning, among children, 27, 29, 92; see also Violence
Fire Department, see Volunteer Fire Departments
Florentine Society, bars Negroes, 64
Folkways (Sumner), 85
Fraternal organizations, barred to Negroes, 37, 63
"Freezing out," white technique of social control, 62, 107-8

Girl Scouts, 35-36; not regarded by Negroes as segregated, 61, 62
Grand Army of the Republic's Women's Relief Corps, barred to Negroes, 64
Grange, barred to Negroes, 63

Habit and tradition, of Negroes maintains race relations pattern, 119-20
Hi-Y, Negro participation in, 36, 116
Home of the Brave, film dealing with race problem, 94
Hotels, Negroes present at conventions and parties, 72; see also Overnight accommodations
Housing, 18, 37, 39-45, 74, 76, 81, 82, 109, 119, 121, 122, 126, 128, 134; discrimination and segregation in, 28-30, 41, 42, 44-45, 75,

92-93, 95-96, 100-2, 105-6, 111-12, 115; condition of, 39-41, 85; neighborhood relations, 30, 45, 60-61, 75, 80, 108, 110; shortage of, 85; white rationalizations for actions, 86-88; white paternalism, 98-99, 118

Ignorance and indifference, on part of whites a form of social control, 109-10, 123; on part of Negro, 131
Ignoring, see Evasion or ignoring
Impersonal factors, maintain race relations pattern, 13-14, 78-85, 123, 135
Indians, slaves in New England before Negroes, 23
Institutional devices, white social control techniques: economic pressure, 95-96; legalistic mechanisms, 96-98; paternalism, 98-100
Insults, see Direct refusal and insult
Irish, in Connecticut Town, 15-16
Italian-American Club, bars Negroes, 64
Italians, in Connecticut Town, 15

Jobs, 18, 46-53, 74, 77, 109, 112-13, 124, 126, 128, 130, 133; majority of Negroes do unskilled or semi-skilled work, 15, 47, 50 ff., 59, 75; discrimination, 26, 30 ff., 46, 47, 48, 49, 50, 51, 52, 53, 88-89, 93-94, 102-4, 105, 106, 107; Negro advancement opportunities limited, 30, 31, 46-47, 50, 53, 79, 82, 106-7, 115, 122; relations between Negro and white workers, 31, 47, 48, 49, 75; domestic service, 40, 53, 75; paternalism on part of management, 47, 49-50, 99, 118 (see also Paternalism); Negroes value jobs for immediate financial return, 47, 81; Negro seniority, 47, 132; see also Unions

Ladies Auxiliary, 36
Lawyers, behavior toward Negroes, 52, 73
Leadership and organization, Negro lack of, 37, 67, 111, 122-23, 124

Legalistic mechanisms, white techniques of social control, 96-98; see also Institutional devices
Lutheran Church, 58
Lutherans, 15, 16

Masons, bar Negroes, 63, 96-97
Methodists, 34, 35
Methodology of study, 18-22
Migration, complete and segmental, a form of Negro avoidance, 111, 124
Mixed dancing, not common, 32, 54-55, 57-58; accepted by whites, 49, 116
Mixed dating, 55, 61; source of annoyance to whites, 33; Negro fear of public opinion prevents, 118
Montclair, New Jersey, "Self-Survey," 100
Mores, of whites, perpetuate race relations pattern, 85-91, 123, 127-28; habit and tradition the Negro counterpart of, 119-20; see also Rationalizations
Movie theater, employment of Negroes, 50-51; discrimination and segregation in, 73-74, 116, 117
Municipal housing project, 115; defeated by whites, 42-43, 67, 98; failure of, indication of white indifference, 109
Musical organizations, Negro participation in, 36, 37, 62-63
Myrdal, G., "Rank Order of Discriminations," 74-75, 91; American Dilemma, 92

Name-calling, 32, 54, 94, 134
National Assn. for the Advancement of Colored People (NAACP), not active in Connecticut Town, 122
Nationality clubs, bar Negroes, 64
Neglect, little on part of Negroes, 66
Nonlocal background, of Negroes, 83-84, 123, 127

Organization, see Leadership and organization
Overnight accommodations, discrimination in, 37, 51, 71-72, 105

Parent Teacher Assn. (PTA), lack of Negro participation in, 56, 76, 80, 116, 122

"Passing" for white, 42, 134

Paternalism, process of white social control, 98-100; affects social and religious activities, 27, 33-34, 57, 58, 63, 65, 72; in jobs, 47, 49-50, 106; Negro desire for, 118, 131; *see also* Institutional devices

"Place" of Negro, 12-13, 19, 94, 123; Negro acceptance of, 33, 129, 130; difficult for newcomers to determine, 38; definition of, not clear, 76-77, 125-26

"Place" of whites, 12-13, 123, 125; *see also* Mores

Police Department, unlikely Negroes could or would join, 37, 66, 82, 89

Politics, 18, 65-68, 74, 96; lack of Negro participation in, 27, 37, 66-67, 76, 79, 80 ff., 104, 108, 114, 116, 122, 126; political favors, 67, 68

Population, Negro, 15, 25, 28, 121; size of, affects prejudices and discriminatory actions, 26, 28, 38, 84-85, 123, 127

Population, white, 15-16

Prejudice, of whites, 62, 84, 107; in housing, 30, 119; alleged, an excuse for discriminatory actions, 103

Pride, Negro, in race, 117-18; personal, 119

Private clubs, 64

Professional men, *see* Dentists, Doctors, Lawyers

Protestant Church, opposes Negro attendance, 59, 75

Protestants, 16; segregated cemetery, 34, 59

Public assistance, little to Negroes, 66

Public facilities, 18, 82-83, 120, 126, 128, 130; discrimination and segregation in, 25, 27, 37, 68-74, 76, 89-90, 94-95, 103-4, 105, 108-9, 111, 114, 116-17, 122, 129, 134

Public opinion, Negro fear of, 118

Public transportation, 74

Public utilities, have never employed Negroes, 52

Race relations, pattern of, 11-12, 18, 79, 91, *et passim;* background of, in Connecticut Town, *1637-1900,* 23-26, *1900-1914,* 26-28, *1914-1950,* 28-38; control and perpetuation of, 12, 85, 120-21, 124, 135; varies with area of behavior, 76, 125-26; Negro acceptance of, 118, 119-23, 124, 129-32; possibility of change in, 132-35

"Rank Order of Discriminations" (Myrdal), 74-75, 91, 135

Rationalizations, used by whites to justify discrimination, 85-91, 92, 123, 128; used by Negroes to justify lack of participation, 117, 122; common to Negroes and whites, 131; *see also* Mores

Rebuff and fear of rebuff, affects Negro behavior, 111-14, 124, 127

Red Cross, lack of Negro participation in, 37, 65, 80, 108, 113

Redmen, bars Negroes, 63, 96-97

Rejection, by whites acts to keep Negroes in "place," 130

Religious activities, *see* Churches, Social and religious activities

Republican Club, 68

Republican Town Committee, 68

Republicans, 43; Connecticut Town tends to be, 67

Responsibility, *see* Dependability or responsibility

Restaurants, discrimination in, 51, 71; why Negroes avoid, 116-17

Restrictions of Negroes, before *1950,* 24

Roman Catholic Church, 15, 17; Negro participation in, 27, 34, 57, 59, 75, 113

Roman Catholics, 16

Roosevelt, Franklin D., antidiscrimination legislation, 31n

Rotary Club, no discrimination, 63

"Run-around," white discriminatory technique, 30, 91, 103

St. Andrews African Methodist Episcopal Zion Church (St. Andrews) 36, 57, 75; paternalistic white support of, 34-35, 100; Negro preference for, 117-18, 120; only Negro institution in Connecticut Town, 121, 122

Schools, 54-57, 76, 77, 122; dicrimination in, 25, 26, 32, 53, 54, 55-56, 94, 107, 132; social and athletic activities, 27, 32-33, 54-55, 60, 82, 116; Negro teachers, 27, 33, 56-57, 76, 88, 104; *see also* Education

Scouting, *see* Boy Scouts, Girl Scouts

Secret organizations, 37

Segregation, historically, 24, 25, 27, 38; pattern of, 76-77, 110; *see also* Housing

Self-segregation, by Negroes, 30, 123, 124, 129-31, 135; rejection of white overtures, 32-33, 37; desire to be with other Negroes, 34-36, 42, 62, 114-18; fear of possible white discriminatory action, 58, 112-14

Sensitivity, of Negroes, 55, 112; imagined slights, 73, 74

Service clubs, admission of Negroes, 37, 63, 97-98

Slavery, 23-25; heritage of, 79

Slavs, in Connecticut Town, 15

Social and religious activities, 18, 57-65, 74, 75, 76, 79, 105; Negro participation in, 27, 30, 35, 37, 48, 49, 54-55, 57-59, 80, 82, 90-91, 96-98, 107-8, 111, 113, 117-18, 122, 126, 127, 129, 131; paternalism in, 57, 63, 65, 99-100, 118

Social clubs, Negro participation in, 37, 108; in churches, 58

Social control, 12-14, 91, 123-24, 125, 126, 131, 134-35; definition of, 14; self-imposed by Negroes, 14, 110, 123, 124 (*see also* Self-segregation); processes and techniques of, 78-124

Socioeconomic status of Negro, 28, 133; cost a factor barring Negro participation, 32, 71, 81, 82; af-fects Negro participation, 35, 37, 58, 72, 76, 126; differences in, from white, 78-83, 134-35

Stereotyping, of Negroes by whites, 28, 87-88, 89, 90; *see also* Rationalizations

Sumner, W. G., *Folkways*, 85; "in-group and out-group," 114

Swedes, in Connecticut Town, 15

Swedish Lodge, bars Negroes, 64

Truman, Harry, antidiscrimination legislation, 31n

Unions, 31, 47, 75; Negro participation in, 32, 48, 49, 79, 81, 113, 119; *see also* Jobs

United Clothing Workers (UCW), 31, 49

United Steelworkers (USW), 31, 32, 47-48, 93, 115

Vested interest, 120-21

Veterans of Foreign Wars, 63-64

Veterans of WW II, 64

Veterans organizations, 37, 63-64

Violence, 12, 91-92, 124, 128, 131; fighting and stoning among children, 27, 29, 92

Visiting Nurse Assn. (VNA), Negroes don't participate in, 37, 65, 80, 108, 113

Volunteer Fire Departments, lack of Negro participation, 37, 65-66, 82, 84, 116; social aspects of, affect Negro exclusions, 65, 97, 98

Voting, Negro, 25, 66

Wirth, L., 130

Women's Republican Club, 68

Women's social clubs, 64-65, 97